D1486950

598.0222 V649
Vezo, Tom.
Wings of spring

MID-CONTINENT PUBLIC LIBRARY
Liberty Branch
1000 Kent Street
Liberty, MO 64068

LI

THIS BOOK WITHDRAWN FROM
THE RECORDS OF THE

FEB 25 2021

MID-CONTINENT PL.

WINGS of SPRING

Courtship, Nesting, and Fledging

PHOTOGRAPHS BY

TOM VEZO

TEXT BY

CHUCK HAGNER

STACKPOLE
BOOKS

MID-CONTINENT PUBLIC LIBRARY

3 0003 00169103 7

MID-CONTINENT PUBLIC LIBRARY
Liberty Branch
1000 Kent Street
Liberty, MO 64068

LI

Photographs copyright ©2006 by Tom Vezo
Text copyright ©2006 by Chuck Hagner

Published by
STACKPOLE BOOKS
5067 Ritter Road, Mechanicsburg, PA 17055
www.stackpolebooks.com

All rights reserved, including the right to reproduce
this book or portions thereof in any form or by
any means, electronic or mechanical, including
photocopying, recording, or by any information
storage and retrieval system without permission in
writing from the publisher. All inquiries should be
addressed to Stackpole Books, 5067 Ritter Road,
Mechanicsburg, PA 17055.

Printed in China

10 9 8 7 6 5 4 3 2 1

First edition

Book design by Larry Lindahl

Library of Congress Cataloging-in-Publication Data

Vezo, Tom.
        Wings of spring / photographs by Tom Vezo ; text by Chuck
    Hagner.— 1st ed.
        p. cm.
    Includes bibliographical references.
    ISBN-13: 978-0-8117-0141-9
    ISBN-10: 0-8117-0141-7
        1. Birds—Behavior. 2. Spring. 3. Birds—Pictorial works. I. Hagner,
    Chuck. II. Title.

QL698.3.V49 2006
598'.022'2—dc22

2005023517

front cover:
Yellow-headed Blackbird
(Xanthocephalus xanthocephalus),
Bear River, UT

back cover:
Great Gray Owl *(Strix nebulosa)*,
Saskatchewan

frontispiece (page ii):
Great Gray Owl *(Strix nebulosa)*,
Saskatchewan

title page (page iii):
Baltimore Oriole *(Icterus galbula)*,
Long Island, NY

page ix:
Snow Goose *(Chen caerulescens)*,
Bosque del Apache National
Wildlife Refuge, NM

Contents

Acknowledgments

I'D LIKE TO ACKNOWLEDGE the following people for their help and support for this book and through my years in photography.

My best friend and wife, Dorothy Vezo, for her constant support and help in my photography.

Donna Fay, my assistant, who works tirelessly in these changing times of technology to make my office run smoothly.

My newfound friends who helped me get some photos for this book, John and Alice Bax and Tony Mercieca. John is a wildlife filmmaker whose work I'd admired for years before I met him. He's made more than twenty films for the Discovery Channel and "Profiles of Nature." I've never photographed with anyone who works harder in the field than John. He possesses an incredible intellect and instinct of the natural world that is extraordinary. I would also like to thank his wife, Alice, who has kept us well fed on the road in Texas and Canada with her wonderful cooking.

Tony Mercieca has been photographing for more than thirty-five years and has been instrumental in improving stop-action flash photography. He builds his own high-speed flash units and was probably the first photographer to create and use the fresnel flash extension. I've had the pleasure of working with these two guys for the past three years and have gained a tremendous amount of knowledge from them.

It was a great pleasure to work with Rob Cavallaro and Mike Whitfield at the Teton Regional Land Trust in Idaho. They work with willing landowners to conserve the best of our fish and wildlife habitats and agricultural lands for future generations.

A special thanks to: Chuck Hagner, who worked hard in researching the facts for this book and putting the text together in wonderfully informative words; Mark Allison, my editor, who believes in my photography and puts up with all my difficult requests; and Larry Lindahl, my good friend who designed this book. Larry designed my last book, *Birds of Prey in the American West*, which won an award in the category of art through the Mountains and Plains Booksellers Association. I was so impressed with his work I asked him to design this book. I worked closely with him through the layout stages of this book and the last one, and I really appreciate his sensitive visual instinct and commonsense graphic design.

This list can go on as so many people have helped in my photographic career, but at the time of this writing I have just returned from the Rio Grande Valley in Texas and would like to acknowledge my good friends there and thank them for their Texas hospitality: Lou and Amalia Powell, Steve Sinclair, Barbara Kennett, Scarlet and George Colley, and everyone at the Laguna Atascosa National Wildlife Refuge.

—T. V.

Finding words to stand up to the images in this book required the generous indulgence and patient support of many people, including Mark Allison at Stackpole; my boss and friend Jim Slocum, vice president for editorial at Kalmbach Publishing Co., publisher of *Birder's World* magazine; my children, James and Ann (who I hope will see in these pages that wonders await them wherever their feet carry them); and especially my wonderful wife, Julie Landes.

—C. H.

"The wilderness *is* therapy."
—Dr. Wayne Dyer

Photographer's Notes

I've been asked many times who has had an influence on my bird photography and the answer struck me about a week after choosing the photos for this project. I was searching through the many photography books I have collected over the years and came across one of my favorites, *The Birds of North America* by Eliot Porter. I remember many years ago, when I first started photographing birds, I would pore over the pages of this book in awe. As I flipped through it again I was amazed to see how much subconscious influence Porter's work has had on my own photography.

What I love most about Porter's bird photographs is how he captured the beauty of these wonderful creatures by including their lifestyles and habitats in his vision. His photos embrace all the beautiful vegetation that surrounds the birds: The old bark and weathered wood of cavity nests add character and realism to his photos. The pine boughs, flower blossoms, branches, and leaves add a third dimension to his photographic paintings. His composition, use of flash, and darkroom techniques show the sensitivity and patience he had in setting up his equipment for that artistic shot. He added spirit, a sense of place, and realism to his images. When you look at them you feel like you are in the photos with the birds.

Inspired by Porter's work, I've tried to achieve the same feeling in my own photography. Although Porter used large-format cameras in controlled nesting conditions for many of his bird photos and most bird photographers today use 35mm equipment, as I do, I always look for the opportunity to compose images that include the beauty of nature. As I've grown in my photography, I've discovered that backgrounds and habitat are as important as the subjects themselves. I feel this adds a third dimension and reality to my images. I've also found that it is essential to be totally immersed in the present when you take pictures—not thinking of the past or the future, what you have to do later, or what you should have done earlier. In that state of mind you are not one hundred percent focused on the creative possibilities your subject offers. You need to slow down your mind and commit to the present to actually see what is around you. I could tell by Porter's photos that this is exactly what he did.

My photography takes me all over the world, and being out in nature is as much a wonderful experience for me as clicking the shutter. Documenting the lives and beauty of birds is a hunt without a gun; it's challenging and exciting, and you never know what images you will come home with. Over time, my interest in the lives of the birds I photograph has expanded considerably. There is so much more to learn about bird behavior, much that is still unknown. This mystery enthralls me.

I've never had any formal photographic training. I learned by reading and by trial and error. I learned by looking at photography books for inspiration and then letting my passion and feelings guide me. I still do. I always try to create a new and different image as I grow and my photographic vision changes.

The photos in this book were taken using both Canon and Nikon 35mm-format equipment. A variety of lenses were used, from a 600mm F4 lens to a wide-angle zoom. My films of choice are Fujichrome Velvia 50 and Provia 100.

I truly hope that the readers of this book will find it interesting and informative. I also hope I can inspire them to pick up a pair of binoculars and observe the beauty of birds and work to protect bird habitat that is being lost daily—not only for the birds, but for all wild animals. Without them we would lose our sense of wonder.

—T. V.

Introduction

DREAM JOB. How else can I describe being the editor of *Birder's World* magazine? For almost my entire life, birds have fascinated and delighted me—their many shapes and sizes; the wide diversity of habitats they occupy; their thickheaded determination to overcome obstacles, natural and man-made; their often stunning beauty; their ability not just to fly but also to soar and swim, dive and hover. No matter which corner of the avian world I inspect, each seems piled high with intellectual and emotional treasure, so much that I have long been convinced that birds would fire my curiosity and fill me with wonder regardless of how I earned a living. I have only to look up.

So how else can you describe editing the leading magazine about wild birds and bird-watching? Six times a year, I get to consider the best places to find birds, how to identify them, and ways to attract them. I have the pleasure of digesting the words of the most experienced and knowledgeable birdwatchers in North America. And best of all, I am privileged to view thousands of photographs of birds captured in all their beauty by photographers like Tom Vezo who are the best in the business.

Like most bird-watchers, I keep a life list, a running tally of all the bird species that I've seen during my lifetime. Many of my friends also maintain state lists, and a few also have county lists, even backyard lists. I should keep a list of species I know only by photograph. Call it a dream list—a roster of birds I look forward to studying through my own binoculars someday. Many of the species Tom included in this book would be on it. Let's hope that the places where he found them will still be wild when I get there.

You'll find more here than just list building, though. Many a bird-watcher has traveled south to the Falkland Islands or Costa Rica or north to Alaska and failed to see the Imperial Shag's

brilliant orange nasal caruncles, the Resplendent Quetzal (with its two-foot-long green plumes) inside a nest cavity, or a clutch of brown Western Sandpiper eggs nestled on the tundra. Such bird-watchers will find these scenes, and hundreds more like them, in these pages.

Like all good photographs, each is valuable for more than its impeccable color, lighting, and composition, more than its beauty, more even than which species is represented. It is valuable for what it reveals. And the photographs collected in this book reveal much that will fire your curiosity and fill you with wonder: the rigors of migration, the rituals that precede pair formation, the wonder of nest construction, strategies that birds use to defeat predators and feed their young, and perhaps most valuable of all, the means by which information essential to the survival of species, true wisdom of the ages, is passed from generation to generation. What words would I use to describe such a publication? Dream book.

—C. H.

FOR ASTRONOMERS and calendar publishers, the first day of spring is cut and dried. But in the avian world, "spring"—the season in which birds migrate, lay eggs, and rear their young—has a wide range of starting dates.

For most North American birds, the wings of spring begin beating in March or April, not long after the vernal equinox. But for some, including Short-eared and Great Horned Owls, breeding season commences in February, January, or even earlier. And for penguins, shags, and other birds of the Southern Hemisphere, spring occurs while we in the North are anticipating winter. What's more, not all birds migrate.

Yet every bird, no matter when its spring begins or how many miles lie between its winter and breeding areas, obeys a universal urge to reproduce. The paths birds follow to achieve this goal are typically arduous—and migration, which is often dangerous and always energy-consuming, is merely the first step. Close on its heels comes a series of equally important challenges, not the least of which are establishing and defending a breeding territory and attracting a mate.

The strategies different birds employ to meet these challenges are as varied as the species themselves. They explain the vivid colors birds sport when courting; they account for an assortment of stereotyped and sometimes spectacular behaviors; and they are a chief reason why, if you're in the right place at the right time, spring can resound with birdsong.

Canada Goose

The annual movement of birds from their winter grounds to the locations where they will mate, lay their eggs, and rear their young is as varied as the birds themselves. For Canada Geese, which breed as far north as Canada's Victoria and Baffin Islands, migration occurs in long lines or V-shaped formations such as this one. Heralds of changing seasons, the passing birds are often heard before they are seen. "One swallow does not make a summer," wrote Aldo Leopold, "but one skein of geese, cleaving the murk of a March thaw, is the spring."

3

Wilson's Snipe

Wilson's Snipe can be found year-round in Rocky Mountain states, and it occasionally spends the winter in northern locales where the ground hasn't frozen, but most of the North American population of the species migrates, and some wintering birds reach South America. By early March, the bird is on the wing again, driven to establish territory on nesting grounds across Canada and in Alaska, the upper Midwest, and the northernmost northeast states, even if the weather there is not yet springlike. This snipe was photographed during a late-June snowstorm in Idaho's Teton Valley, where the species lives year-round. The bird is holding one leg close to its body, a behavior that helps it conserve heat.

Short-eared Owl

The Short-eared Owl inhabits marshes, grasslands, and tundra throughout much of North America and Eurasia, as well as South American grasslands and the Hawaiian and Galapagos Islands. The species begins its reproductive efforts even earlier than Wilson's Snipe. As early as mid-February, males attempt to woo mates by means of a conspicuous sky dance, or courtship flight. As a perched female looks on, the male owl flies upward in tight circles, hangs in the wind and hoots, then dives, clapping its wings together beneath its body. If receptive, the female will chase after the male as he passes.

Long-billed Curlew

Among the eight curlews that have been recorded in North America are some of the most storied species in the world. One, the rare Bristle-thighed Curlew, is famous for its long-distance migration. Each year it flies from nesting grounds in western Alaska to Hawaii and other Pacific islands—a distance of twenty-five hundred miles nonstop. Another, the Eskimo Curlew, may have been hunted into extinction as it migrated between Argentina and the Arctic; the last confirmed sighting of the species was in 1963. The extraordinary and aptly named Long-billed Curlew, pictured here, is the only curlew to nest in the continental United States.

Wilson's Warbler is one of many colorful songbirds whose appearance in spring signals the end of winter in North America. The lemon-yellow, black-capped wood-warbler winters in southern Louisiana and from extreme southern Texas to Costa Rica and Panama; it does not cross the Gulf of Mexico as it migrates northward. The bird times its northern migration to arrive in the coastal and boreal forests of North America just as they turn green and come alive with the bees, flies, mayflies, spiders, and beetles that make up the bird's diet during breeding season.

Dowitchers

The epic sweep of migration is most easily appreciated at mudflats on both coasts of North America and shallow bodies of water in the continent's interior. Year after year, shorebirds such as the dowitchers pictured here gather at these locations in large, often spectacularly huge, flocks to rest and feed before continuing north to breeding areas in distant Canada, Alaska, even Russia. The two dowitcher species that occur in North America, Short-billed and Long-billed, look nearly identical; they are best distinguished by their flight calls.

Crested
Caracara

The Crested Caracara resides throughout Central
and South America and as far south as Tierra del
Fuego but occurs in the United States only in
southern Arizona, southeastern Texas, and south-
central Florida, where it is listed as threatened.
A bird of wide-open spaces, the caracara likes to
be able to observe its surroundings, so it invariably
constructs its nest in the tallest vegetation around.
In Florida, this is usually a cabbage palm. In
Arizona, it's often a large saguaro cactus. In Texas,
caracaras prefer live oak or elm trees. This bird,
in the Rio Grande Valley, is resting on a yucca.

Willow Ptarmigan

Willow Ptarmigan, one of a trio of ptarmigans that occur in North America, wears three distinct plumages throughout the year so it always blends with the ever-changing colors of its extreme northern surroundings. In winter, when it is not breeding and its surroundings are blanketed with snow, all of the bird's feathers except its tail are pure white. In springtime, when patches of vegetation emerge from melting snow, red-brown feathers grow on the ptarmigan's head and neck. By midsummer, adult male ptarmigans look like this bird—only its belly and wing feathers are still white.

Brown Pelican

The dark brown feathers on these Brown Pelicans' necks appear only during the courting season. Brown Pelicans can be found year-round along the Pacific, Atlantic, and Gulf coasts; in the Gulf of California and the Caribbean; and in isolated locations as far south as Ecuador and the Galapagos Islands. Caribbean pelicans are smaller than Gulf and Atlantic birds, and Pacific pelicans, like this pair, are the largest. The vivid red of the birds' pouches further distinguishes them as members of the Pacific subspecies.

American White Pelican

American White Pelicans are social birds. They nest in colonies, frequently forage as a group, and make their long annual migrations from winter grounds in California, the Gulf states, Mexico, and Nicaragua to breeding areas in the Dakotas, Alberta, Saskatchewan, and Manitoba in flocks. They often arrange themselves in long lines or V- or J-shaped formations as they fly. As each pelican rises or descends to match the movements of the bird ahead of it, the airborne formation appears to undulate like a wave.

Rufous Hummingbird

Scientists have named more than 320 species of hummingbirds, all of which occur in the Americas. This penny-colored male Rufous Hummingbird, photographed near Tucson, Arizona, is one of seventeen species that have bred in the United States and Canada. Its throat looks dark, but the feathers between its bill and white chest are iridescent, capable of gleaming a brilliant metallic orange-scarlet. The color becomes visible only when the bird and its observer, human or avian, are positioned just right. Male hummingbirds make use of their vivid colors to drive other males out of their territories and impress eligible females during mating season.

Rufous-tailed Hummingbird

The Rufous-tailed Hummingbird, a common resident of the humid tropics, is found from northwestern South America to eastern Mexico. It is a member of the genus *Amazilia* and so is a relative of the Berylline, Buff-bellied, and Violet-crowned Hummingbirds treasured by birdwatchers in the southern and southwestern United States, but it has been reported only once or twice in southern Texas. It nests almost year-round.

Scintillant Hummingbird

This tiny Scintillant Hummingbird, a member of the genus *Selasphorus,* is tropical kin to the familiar Broad-billed, Rufous, and Allen's Hummingbirds of North America. Like the males of these species, the male scintillant will dive at rivals that enter its mating territory and attempt to chase them away. When it does, air rushing between the tapered tips of its primary feathers produces a shrill cicadalike whistle that ornithologists believe not only intimidates other males but also entices females.

Indigo
Bunting

The completeness of this male Indigo Bunting's radiant blue coloration indicates that the bird has completed at least two trips from wintering grounds in southern Florida, the Caribbean, Mexico, or Central America. The plumages of males that hatched the previous spring and are making their first trip to their breeding grounds look noticeably different. Far from all blue, they can be as much as eighty percent brownish and white. Indigo Buntings establish territory by singing and chasing neighboring males. The older males often replace younger males; nearly all of them attract females.

Nashville Warbler

Warblers, despite their name, don't warble. Instead, most species produce a thin, lispy note while flying in a flock; a sharp, clear call note when agitated; and a variety of not-very-musical songs that often include trills. The male Nashville Warbler has two types of song: One it uses during the day to attract a mate. The other, which the bird typically gives at dawn, is for communicating with other males. The small patch of chestnut-colored feathers on the top of this bird's head is exceptionally difficult to see in the field.

Marsh Wren

Male Marsh Wrens are busy birds each spring. Not only do they commonly build as many as twenty dummy nests that no female will ever lay eggs in, they also sing day and night, cycling through a repertoire that can include more than two hundred different songs. Males commence singing a day or two after arriving on their breeding territories and, unlike other songbirds, increase their singing after they have attracted a mate and continue to sing during laying and incubation. In some Marsh Wren populations, more than half the males mate with two or more females.

Painted Bunting

Like Indigo Buntings, male Painted Buntings do not exhibit their most spectacular colors until their second breeding season. Then they are a feast for the eyes: The bird's head and neck are rich blue; feathers on its back are bright yellowish green; and its chin, breast, undersides, and rump are red. Moreover, a narrow ring of vermilion highlights each eye. The bunting's beauty comes at a steep price, however. Painted Buntings are popular cage birds, especially in Asia and Europe, and they are captured for export in high numbers on their wintering grounds in Mexico, Central America, and the Caribbean.

Baltimore Oriole

The icterid family includes the all-black blackbirds, grackles, and cowbirds as well as the colorful orioles: the lemon-yellow Audubon's and Scott's Orioles; the chestnut-colored Orchard Oriole; and the orange Hooded, Bullock's, Spot-breasted, Altamira, and Baltimore Orioles. The brilliant color on this male Baltimore Oriole isn't limited to its breast and belly. The bird's rump and undertail coverts are also orange, as are the upper and lower sides of its tail. The oriole also has orange underwings and shoulders.

Green Jay

With the exception of Clark's Nutcracker and Gray Jay, North America's jays are mostly blue. This sets them apart from Old World family members, which are mostly gray, brown, or iridescent, and makes this beautiful Green Jay even more noteworthy. It and the Brown Jay are our only two tropical jays. Both are found in the United States only in south Texas, and both have a unique patch of stiffened feathers between their bills and eyes. On the Brown Jay these are brown, on the Green Jay deep blue.

Northern Cardinal

All male Northern Cardinals are red, but some cardinals are brighter than others. The reason, ornithologists are learning, has to do with the varying amounts of red carotenoid pigments the birds obtain from their diet during their annual molt. Birds that eat more carotenoid-rich food when they shed their worn feathers deposit more of the pigments in their new feathers, so the birds appear redder when they arrive on their breeding grounds. Brighter males have been shown to hold territories with denser vegetation and have greater reproductive success than paler males.

Wood Duck

The Wood Duck is as distinctive as it is colorful, but it doesn't wear its unique plumage all year. Shortly after breeding, the duck sheds and replaces all its feathers. The rakish crest disappears. The iridescent green, blue, and violet head feathers are replaced with new plumage that is mostly gray. And the purplish chestnut breast, the white and black bars that border it, and the bird's yellow-gold flanks all go brownish gray. The drab raiment, known as eclipse plumage, is worn for only several weeks. Then, between July and early September, the bird molts again, and the duck's familiar color scheme is restored.

Resplendent Quetzal

A bristly green crest, maroon chest, and crimson belly make the male Resplendent Quetzal, a relative of the Elegant Trogon of southeastern Arizona, one of the most stunning birds in tropical America. It resides in cloud and montane forests from southern Mexico to western Panama. Elongated upper tail coverts extend beyond the bird's snow-white tail feathers, forming streamers that can grow more than two feet long on the male and wave in the air when it flies.

Crimson-collared Tanager

The Crimson-collared Tanager can be found along the Gulf-Caribbean slope from Veracruz, Oaxaca, Tabasco, and Chiapas in southern Mexico southeast through Guatemala and Belize to Costa Rica and Panama. The red-eyed, silver-billed songbird is one of more than two hundred tanagers and honeycreepers in the family Thraupidae, the overwhelming majority of which live in the New World tropics. Only a handful occur in temperate North America.

Yellow-headed Blackbird

Audubon referred to the "croaking note" of the Yellow-headed Blackbird as a "compound, not to be mistaken, between that of the Crow Blackbird and that of the Red winged Starling." Tail lowered, wings spread enough to expose bright white primary coverts, and head tilted upward, this male near Salt Lake City, Utah, is directing such a note toward a distant bird, as either a warning to a male that flew over its territory or a how-do-you-do to a just-arrived female. Highly social, Yellow-headed Blackbirds nest in loose colonies, and males defend their territories vigorously, often displacing Red-winged Blackbirds that have established territories nearby.

This portrait makes plain why the handsome Imperial Shag is also known as the blue-eyed shag. The bird is a member of the same family as the all-dark cormorants of North America, but it lives in a world apart: the southernmost tip of South America, the Falkland Islands, and the fringes of Antarctica, where this photo was taken. Like most cormorants of the Southern Hemisphere, the Imperial Shag has bright white underparts. This shag has grown a crest, and its nasal caruncles are enlarged and intensely orange, indicators that the bird is ready for courting.

Gambel's Quail

Secretive, chickenlike Gambel's Quail occurs year-round in Arizona and the northwestern part of the adjacent Mexican state of Sonora. In hopes of winning a mate during breeding season, dark-bellied, black-faced males like this one chase and nudge hens in their coveys, then woo prospective mates by making highly ritualized offerings of food to them. As they do, the males hold their fanned tails high and their bills close to the ground, bowing and bobbing their topknot-adorned heads and flashing their yellow and black belly patches.

Green Heron

A history of name changes—from Green Heron to Green-backed Heron and back again—draws attention to the striking plumes that adorn the back of this species, but it is the unfeathered parts of the bird that tell the whole story. They reveal that this heron was photographed near the height of breeding season. The bill is glossy black; at other times, the lower mandible is dusky green and yellowish at the base. The lore, the area between the bill and eyes, has likewise turned bluish black; normally it is dull yellow-green and blackish. And this bird's legs are orange; on nonbreeding adults, they're yellow or orange-yellow.

Great Blue Heron

Of the thirteen herons, egrets, and bitterns that breed in North America, the Great Blue Heron is the largest, and its many spectacular breeding displays are arguably the most thrilling to observe. This pair was photographed in Florida as they were completing an elaborate greeting ceremony. Both herons have fully erected their neck plumes and are holding their bills nearly horizontal in a fluffed-neck display. The unfeathered parts of both birds show heightened colors that will fade soon after egg laying begins: bright cobalt-blue lores, yellow-orange bills, reddish legs, and deep yellow eyes.

Ring-necked Pheasant

The Ring-necked Pheasant is not native to North America. It was introduced here, and to every other continent except Antarctica, and since the late 1930s has become abundant in corn- and grain-producing areas from coast to coast. This drake was photographed on Long Island as it performed a courtship display. Walking toward a hen, the bird holds its head high, the better to show the bright red skin around its eyes and bill and the dark, hornlike pinnae on top of its head. The pheasant has also spread its long tail feathers and is lifting its wings, revealing dazzling golden-yellow flanks.

Pacific Loon

Like the four other loons that breed in North America, the Pacific Loon replaces its plain-looking gray and white winter plumage between February and May so that its appearance is dazzling come breeding time. Jet-black feathers take the place of white ones on its chin and throat, satiny silver-gray feathers cover its crown and nape, and stark white patches appear on its black back. This bird was photographed in Churchill, Manitoba, near the southeastern limit of its breeding range, as it was rearing up out of the water— a predator, a jaeger, was flying overhead.

Northern Gannet

All the world's Northern Gannets breed in one of only thirty-eight colonies, the majority of which are located in the eastern North Atlantic: in northwest France, the British Isles, Iceland, the Faeroe Islands, and Norway. Six colonies are in North America, all in Canada: three on islands in the Gulf of St. Lawrence, and three in nearby Newfoundland. The photo at left was taken at Cape St. Mary's, on the Avalon Peninsula, Newfoundland, where gannets gather every year in spectacular numbers, claiming almost every bit of space on the mainland's sheer cliffs and a towering rock stack just offshore.

Cod in the North Sea, capelin off the coast of Norway, mackerel and herring in the shallow waters of the continental shelf off North America . . . the ability to reach such resources efficiently is a crucial factor in where the fish-eating gannet locates its nest. So too is a safe distance from foxes, weasels, and other potential predators. The bird above is demonstrating yet another quality of a good nest site: an abundance of nearly continuous wind to assist with takeoffs and landings.

This pair of Northern Gannets, photographed at Cape St. Mary's, are breeding adults. Overall, they are clean white, but champagne-yellow feathers highlight the birds' crowns, sides of their heads, and napes, and black primary feathers can be seen at the tips of their folded wings. The gannets' dapper coloration reveals that they are in at least their third or fourth year. Younger birds would show a highly variable mix of white and black on their tails, backs, and wings—and there is little chance that a younger male would be able to win breeding territory.

Laughing Gull

Male and female Laughing Gulls are indistinguishable. In breeding plumage, both sexes have black heads, white crescents above and below the eyes, and red bills. Yet the female in this photo, taken while two birds were courting, is easy to spot. Facing the male, she has pulled her head down onto her body so she appears smaller and more compact than he does. From this position, she will signal her acceptance of her mate with a head toss, and he will ceremoniously regurgitate partially digested food for her. After she eats it, they will mate.

King Penguin

King Penguins are highly gregarious when breeding. Each year, between November and April, they gather on beaches and in ice- and snow-free valleys on Marion, Prince Edward, Crozet, and other subantarctic islands and form dense breeding colonies consisting of many tens of thousands of birds. The immense colony pictured here is on South Georgia Island in the South Atlantic, about eleven hundred miles east of Tierra del Fuego. The King Penguin does not make a nest, and it lays only one egg. To keep it warm, the bird cradles it on the tops of its feet and presses it against an unfeathered patch of skin located low on its belly.

With the exception of the warm-weather Galapagos Penguin, which breeds on both sides of the equator, all the world's penguins live in the Southern Hemisphere, and many occur where it can be very cold. Like all birds, penguins depend upon their feathers to repel water and trap body heat, so they preen constantly, and a number of penguins preen each other as shown below. Known as allopreening, this behavior allows birds to control ticks and fleas. For species like King Penguins, which breed in locations far too cold for such parasites, allopreening's other purpose—maintaining and strengthening the pair bond—is more important.

Parakeet Auklet

Four of the six auklets that breed in North America can be found year-round in the Bering Sea region. The white-eyed Parakeet Auklet has the widest distribution, nesting on Russia's Kuril Islands, in the Sea of Okhotsk, and along the Kamchatka peninsula as well as along south coastal Alaska. This pair was photographed on St. Paul, one of Alaska's Pribilof Islands, while they were courting. Attracted by the male's whinnying advertisements, the female crouches before him, her poppy-red bill almost touching his. Once their pair bond has been formed on land, the birds will mate at sea.

Tufted Puffin

Tufted Puffins nest in one of 1,031 known colonies. Many of these are in Asia, scattered along the Chukchi and Kamchatka peninsulas and in the Sea of Okhotsk in northeast Russia, but the majority, 802 colonies, are on islands off the coasts of California, Oregon, Washington, British Columbia, and Alaska. The pair at left is near their nest in a colony on St. Paul. Tufted Puffins typically nest in earthen burrows, which they excavate on steep, lushly vegetated slopes. Such nests are usually occupied by the same birds year after year.

Puffins defend their nest burrows aggressively, and not just against other species. Even when other Tufted Puffins come near, the territory holders will respond with stereotyped threat displays intended to make intruders stay away. In the photo above, taken just after the arrival of the puffin on the right, the bird on the left has adopted what ornithologists call a forward-threat posture. Its head is down, its bill is closed, its wings are spread, and it is directly facing the newcomer. If the display were ignored, violence could follow.

Atlantic Puffin

Just as Tufted and Horned Puffins enliven the northwestern edge of the continent, the Atlantic Puffin brightens the northeast. It breeds along the coast of Greenland, at Witless Bay in Newfoundland, along the north shore of the Gulf of St. Lawrence, and at other locations in eastern Canada and Maine. Since 1973 it has been successfully reintroduced on Maine's East Egg Rock and at the Seal Island National Wildlife Refuge, in outer Penobscot Bay. This pair was photographed at Machias Seal Island, the only North American puffin colony where tourists are allowed to observe the birds from close range.

Black-browed Albatross

Two Black-browed Albatrosses briefly hold their bills close together during a courtship display. The act is the culmination of a series of gestures aimed at establishing familiarity. Long-winged aviators of windswept oceans around the world, albatrosses make their way to either coast of North America usually by accident—only two, the Black-footed and Laysan Albatrosses, occur regularly. They and the Short-tailed Albatross nest in the North Pacific. The Waved Albatross lives along the equator. All the rest, including the Black-browed Albatross, live in the remote Southern Hemisphere.

Common Tern

Courtship complete, this pair of Common Terns copulates on their nesting territory on Long Island. Fish are the tern's primary food, and fish play an important role in the bird's breeding behavior. Early in courtship, a male tern will advertise for a mate by approaching a female and offering a fish to her. Later, after the pair has established a bond, the female will join him on his feeding territory but make little or no effort to catch food for herself. Instead, she will wait for the male to deliver fish to her. Such courtship feeding helps females increase body mass before egg laying.

Common Moorhen

All birds excrete waste, copulate, and lay eggs via a single opening called the cloaca, which is located under their tails. These Common Moorhens are copulating. The male is standing on the female's back and curling his tail downward to make his cloaca touch hers. Sperm transferred from him will swim directly from the female's cloaca to the upper end of her oviduct, where they may encounter an ovum and fertilize it. Fertilization converts the ovum into an embryo and starts the process by which it would gain egg whites, a hard outer shell, and pigmentation before it is laid. Moorhens typically lay eight to eleven eggs.

Anhinga

Because the Anhinga's striking black and white feathers become waterlogged easily as it swims in search of fish to eat, the familiar "snake bird" is often seen perched in this posture. Holding its wings spread, this male is letting the bright Florida sunshine dry its soaked plumage and warm its slender body. The vivid orange-yellow hue of the Anhinga's bill, the iridescent green of the bare skin around and below its eyes, and the faint whitish plumes on the sides of its crown, nape, and upper neck all indicate that the bird is in breeding plumage.

Black-bellied Whistling-Duck

Of the world's eight whistling-duck species, only the Fulvous and Black-bellied breed in North America. The Black-bellied Whistling-Duck also breeds in coastal Central America and as far south as Peru, Paraguay, and northern Argentina. But in North America, for the most part, it's limited to southeastern Arizona and southeastern Texas. The pink-billed birds nest primarily in natural cavities in trees, but they also use nest boxes. It is believed that the birds pair up before they arrive on their breeding grounds and that their pair bond lasts a lifetime.

Wandering Albatross

Wandering Albatrosses are well known as loud dancers. When courting, they extend their heads and necks rigidly toward their partners. They rotate their bills up to near vertical and curl their necks backward. They vibrate their upper and lower mandibles, producing a drumming sound. And, after fanning their tails and spreading their wings, they jut out their breasts, swing their heads straight up, and scream. The birds perform these stereotyped behaviors in pairs as well as on chaotic communal dancing grounds, where partners can change constantly. Males that manage to hold the attention of a female typically attempt to lead her away from the other birds, frequently to a nest site.

All albatrosses gather nesting materials, but characteristically they do not walk with them. Instead, from a position on or near the nest site, the birds use their bills to yank up only the loose vegetation and mud that is within reach and then toss or place it to one side in a stereotyped over-the-shoulder motion. The pair of Wandering Albatrosses below is forming a mound among tussocks of grass. When they are finished, their nest will be about three feet in diameter and stand more than a foot tall. The birds will add new material to it throughout the year.

Macaroni Penguin

These orange-plumed Macaroni Penguins were photographed at their nest site in Antarctica. Macaronis typically lay two eggs, one four days after the other, but the first almost never survives. Even though the embryo inside is viable, in most cases the first egg is discarded before the second egg is laid. And even when the first egg is not lost, the second is still favored. Macaronis don't start incubating until the second egg is laid, and the second is always bigger and heavier than the first, so the second embryo is more likely to hatch than the first; it requires less time to become strong enough to break out of its shell.

Least Auklet

The process by which Least Auklets become a pair begins with stereotyped chattering by the male. An interested female will respond by extending her neck and staring intently, then she will raise her nape feathers and lean forward until her head and body are at the same height. If the male also leans forward and chatters, the female will cautiously touch his neck, face, or bill with her bill. Then both birds will chatter in duet while the female nibbles on the male's bill. The combined chattering of many auklets can be heard a mile away from a large breeding colony. This pair was photographed amid the clamor on the Pribilof Islands.

Great Egret

This male Great Egret has already selected a nest site and begun to build a nest platform. Now, with dozens of long, wispy plumes known as aigrettes standing erect on its back, the bird is lowering its head toward its back in a stereotyped stretching display intended to attract a mate. The bright orange-yellow of the egret's bill and the lime green of the unfeathered area between the eyes and bill occur only during breeding season. The bird will shed the aigrettes in the summer or early fall.

Male egrets always select the nest site, pick nesting materials, and start building before they turn their attention to attracting a mate. The locations the males choose for the nests, typically near the top of a tree or shrub and exposed not only from above but also on one side, make excellent stages for their courtship displays. After pair formation, their mates often help them complete construction of the platform.

BIRDS MUST MAKE a life-and-death decision after they have acquired their breeding territories: they must choose the exact location for their nest. Much rides on the selection, because most birds breed in regions that are subject to harsh weather or are inhabited by predatory animals—including other birds.

A nest constructed too low in a shrub or tree might be an easy mark for a fox or coyote while one situated in direct sunlight might be too hot for embryos inside eggs to develop properly. And a nest that is poorly camouflaged could put the adult as well as the eggs at risk. The successful nest shelters not only the eggs, but also the bird that incubates them.

Satisfying both requirements can be challenging, but birds have found more than one way to succeed. Roadrunners, for example, nest in the predator-discouraging and shade-providing arms of cholla cacti. Ovenbirds incubate in leafy domes cleverly hidden on the forest floor. Swallows retreat to mud nests affixed to high walls; grebes to sodden mounds surrounded on all sides by water, puffins, auklets, and Burrowing Owls to holes in the ground.

The birds' ingenuity renders all the more astonishing the large number of species—gulls, boobies, penguins, sandpipers, terns, and others—that lay their eggs in little more than scrapes in the earth. Located in plain view of potential predators, exposed to the elements, and sparsely lined, the nests seem insufficient but in fact lack nothing.

Herring Gull

The Herring Gull is perhaps the most widespread gull in North America. It nests in colonies along the Atlantic coast, around the Great Lakes, and in the north from Newfoundland to Alaska. Both members of a Herring Gull pair typically dig and line three or four shallow scrapes, locating them next to a bush or other windbreak. Each gull then displays over each nest it completes. If its mate responds by displaying the same way, the nest site is chosen.

Sex roles are reversed in phalaropes: The female wears the brightly colored plumage, and the male incubates the eggs and cares for the young. This bird, a male, is a Wilson's Phalarope, one of three phalaropes that occur in North America and the only one that does not breed on arctic tundra. It nests instead on the northern Great Plains. This photo was taken at the Bear River Migratory Bird Refuge in Utah as the phalarope sat on eggs in its nest and tugged on the surrounding grasses to form a canopy.

Greater Roadrunner

The Greater Roadrunner is a member of the cuckoo family, along with Black-billed, Yellow-billed, and Mangrove Cuckoos; anis; and two Old World cuckoos that turn up in North America only accidentally. Well known across a wide area of the Southwest, it can be found year-round from southern California to Louisiana and as far south as Michoacan in Mexico, where its range overlaps that of the more southerly Lesser Roadrunner. Like parrots and most woodpeckers, roadrunners have zygodactyl feet. Two of their four toes point forward, and two point backward, so the bird leaves a distinctive X-shaped track as it walks.

The Greater Roadrunner at top has chosen the location of its nest well. Located at least three feet high and near the center of a prickly cholla cactus, the platform of sticks is out of the reach of most coyotes, raccoons, skunks, and other mammalian predators. They can get to only low branches, and the cactus's abundant thorns will make them think twice about climbing. The nest's internal location also guarantees that the plant will at least partly block the hot desert sun, providing shade to keep nestlings cool and helping conceal the incubating parent by bathing it in dappled light.

Great Horned Owl

The remarkable Great Horned Owl can be found year-round from coast to coast and from the northern limits of the boreal forest to the deserts of Mexico. Its diet is the broadest of any North American owl, and it nests in a wider range of sites than any other bird in the Americas. While it prefers to occupy the stick structures that hawks and eagles have left in trees, it also nests in tree hollows and snags, on broken limbs, in old squirrel nests, on cliff faces and rock outcrops, even on the ground. This owl has chosen a sycamore tree in Peppersauce Canyon, Arizona.

Great Horned Owls breed early in the year. In Wisconsin they hoot vigorously and start inspecting potential nest sites as early as January, and owls in more southerly locations, like this one in Arizona, start even earlier. Here a female and her young have usurped a stick nest built by a hawk in a saguaro cactus. Essentially naked and immobile at hatching, the owlets keep their eyes closed for the first nine or ten days but develop quickly. By the time they are seven weeks old, the birds will be fully feathered and capable of flight.

Harris's Hawk

Like other species of birds of prey, the
Harris's Hawk builds a substantial
nest of sticks, usually in a mesquite or
paloverde tree but often in the location
shown here—between the up-reaching
arms of a giant saguaro cactus. Extremely
social by nature, Harris's Hawks nest in
cooperative groups that can include as
many as seven birds, including both
adults and offspring that associate with
their parents for up to three years. Group
members help the parents care for and
defend nestlings and participate in
sophisticated cooperative hunting forays.

Scott's Oriole

The dead leaves that hang beneath the living crown of many yucca trees in the Southwest are important to Scott's Orioles. The females visit the trees each April and strip long, stringy fibers from the dead leaves' edges. They then weave the fibers together to form the main part of their hanging nests, typically a round or oval basket attached on one side to overhanging leaves at the top of a yucca. This bright yellow, black, and white male Scott's Oriole has returned with an insect to a nest in Madera Canyon, Arizona.

The tiny, yellow-headed Verdin can be found year-round from southern California to central Texas and south to Baja California and central Mexico. This bird in Green Valley, Arizona, is perched at the entrance to its ball-shaped nest. Verdins build one or two breeding nests in the spring and several roosting nests throughout the year. Prickly looking on the outside, the carefully constructed seven-inch breeding nests have a soft inner cavity lined with leaves, grasses, plant down, and feathers from quail, doves, and other birds, all bound together with spider silk. Roosting nests look similar but are smaller.

This male Resplendent Quetzal is clinging
to the trunk of a tree near the entrance
to its nest. Like many owls, woodpeckers,
flycatchers, chickadees, wrens, and other
birds, the tropical quetzal is a cavity-nesting
species. It lays its eggs in voids in decaying
trees or stumps, in old woodpecker holes,
and occasionally in abandoned termite
mounds. Both adults help excavate the
cavity, and the male, despite his elaborate
green plumes, takes his turn incubating.

Black-faced Solitaire

This adult Black-faced Solitaire, a secretive highland species of Costa Rica and western Panama, is standing on the rim of a cup-shaped nest constructed of mosses and rootlets. Like the Wood Thrush and other members of the large thrush family, it is an accomplished singer whose flutelike song has been described as "one of the most magical sounds in Costa Rica's mountain forests."

Burrowing Owl

Leaning forward and daring, this Burrowing Owl makes no bones about its intention to defend the nest burrow behind it. The owl breeds on dry, treeless plains in southern Canada and across much of the western United States and Mexico, where it occupies the burrows of prairie dogs, ground squirrels, and other animals. It also breeds in Florida, where it often digs its own burrows.

Burrowing Owls will adorn the entrances with shells, shredded paper, tinfoil, and other objects and may line the openings with dried cow and horse manure. The dung attracts beetles that the owls eat, and the odor is thought to keep predators from detecting the birds' scent.

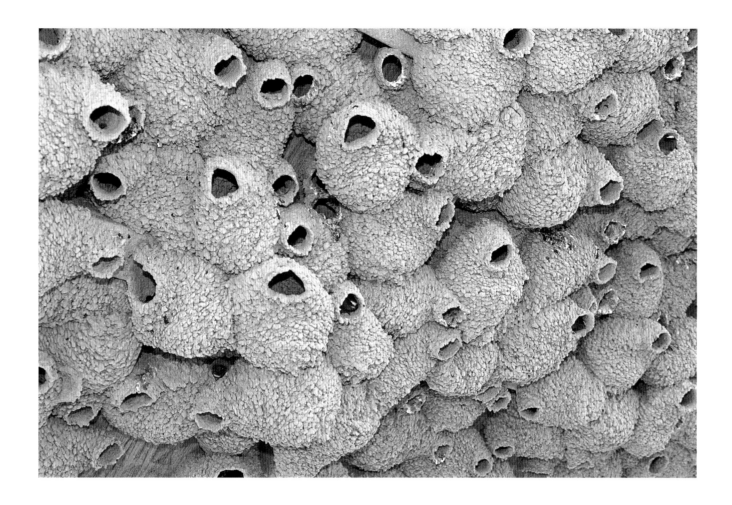

Cliff Swallow

Among the eight swallows that breed in North America, only Cliff, Cave, and Barn Swallows make their nests of mud, and the Cliff Swallow is the master builder of the group, as the photo above makes clear. Each Cliff Swallow nest is a gourd-shaped enclosure constructed of nine- to twelve-hundred tiny mud pellets that the bird transports one by one to the nest site and then presses into place with its bill. Extremely social, Cliff Swallows often form colonies containing hundreds of nests. They remain in large flocks outside of breeding season.

Cliff Swallows always face out when they sit in the entrances to their nests, and with good reason: Other swallows may attempt

to build directly below their nests, blocking the entrances, and neighboring swallows will steal wet mud from unattended nests. Worse, Cliff Swallows lay eggs in their neighbors' nests or move eggs from their own nest into the neighbor's. These acts of brood parasitism happen so frequently that researchers say up to forty-three percent of Cliff Swallow nests in Nebraska contain at least one nestling that is not related genetically to one or either parent.

All birds must keep their eggs within a narrow temperature range in order for the embryos inside to develop properly. If temperatures rise above 104.9 degrees F or fall below 78.8 degrees, the embryos will die, and even short exposures to temperatures between 78.8 degrees and 95 degrees can disrupt development. Most birds transfer heat to their eggs through bare patches of skin on the abdomen or breast called brood patches, but boobies lack them. Instead, like this Masked Booby, they incubate by laying their feet on their eggs.

Chinstrap Penguin

The Chinstrap Penguin gets it name from the narrow band of black feathers that separates its chin from its throat and runs from ear to ear. The thin black slit visible behind the bill of this bird is one of its closed eyes; this photo was taken in a breeding colony on South Georgia Island while the penguin was dozing. It is sitting on two eggs, which both parents will incubate. The eggs will hatch in thirty-four to thirty-six days.

Gentoo Penguin

The Gentoo Penguin nests mainly on subantarctic islands, but its range extends to the Antarctic Peninsula, so it can be counted among the four penguin species that breed on the frozen continent. (Emperor, Chinstrap, and Adelie Penguins are the other three.) The Gentoos visible here are lying on simple nests that are little more than scrapes in the ground lined with mounded stones and perhaps feathers, shells, or bones. Females lay two eggs but typically go to sea for a day or two between laying them. The first is more likely to survive when feeding conditions are poor.

Imperial Shag

Shags typically construct their nest mounds on the tops of flat rocks or on small islands in seas or lakes, and they always nest in colonies. A small colony is shown at right; other colonies can be much larger and far more densely populated affairs, involving as many as hundreds of thousands of birds. Shags reuse the colonies year after year. Local residents told researchers that one Imperial Shag colony on the northwest corner of Tierra del Fuego had been in existence for no less than fifty years, and probably longer.

The shag constructs one of the most unusual nests in the bird world. A large, solid mound of dried seaweed, caked mud, and guano, it represents the weathered end-product of many dives to nearby shallow sea bottoms and frequent flights to seaweed-littered beaches. It is also the subject of near-constant renovation and rearranging, activities that occur even after egg laying begins. The shag pictured below is resting in a shallow depression, freshly lined with seaweed, that shelters a clutch of precious eggs.

Black-browed Albatrosses breed in colonies that can vary in
size from fewer than ten pairs of birds to more than a hundred
thousand. This nest is typical. Situated on the Falkland Islands
on a slope only a short distance from the expanse of sea in the
background, it consists of mud and peat (and perhaps the bones
of chicks that died in years past). The albatross has fashioned the
materials into a stout and resilient column about sixteen inches
in diameter and seven to fourteen inches tall. The bird is sitting
on an egg in a shallow depression at the nest's top.

Parakeet Auklet

Like guillemots, puffins, and other auks, Parakeet Auklets spend almost their entire lives at sea. They come to land only to breed. While Parakeet Auklets have been known to make their nests in burrows that were excavated by Cassin's Auklets, Tufted Puffins, or Ancient Murrelets, or in burrows they dug themselves, this bird did neither. It is loafing outside a naturally occurring cavity on St. Paul Island, Alaska. The Parakeet Auklet brings no seaweed, grass, or other materials to line its nest. Instead, it lays its single egg on the bare floor of the cavity. Both adults share incubation duties.

American Golden-Plover

The five-ounce American Golden-Plover spends the winter far below the equator but nests on arctic and subarctic tundra near the top of the world. This bird and its four speckled eggs were photographed in Manitoba, end point of a northward migration that covered more than six thousand miles and took three months.

Most golden-plovers leave Bolivia, Paraguay, southern Brazil, Uruguay, and Argentina—their primary winter range—in February and arrive in northern North America between mid-May and early June. Some adults will begin their return flight only a few weeks later, but most depart in August.

How much camouflage a bird egg possesses generally conforms to how readily a potential predator might spot it. Eggs laid in cavities or burrows are out of sight and need no camouflage; they are usually dull white. But the Dunlin eggs pictured here are different. Nestled in a simple depression on the Canadian tundra, they lie where any hungry arctic or red fox or weasel would surely spot them if they were white. But they are the color of grass, and they are marked with brownish black splotches that make the eggs blend in with the surrounding vegetation.

Each spring, before Western Sandpipers arrive on their breeding grounds in southwestern and extreme northern Alaska, the Seward Peninsula, and eastern Siberia, they often stop to rest and feed in huge, spectacular flocks in San Francisco Bay, Washington State's Grays Harbor, the Fraser River Delta in British Columbia, and the Stikine and Copper River deltas in south coastal Alaska. Male sandpipers typically arrive on the breeding grounds before females to establish territories. Egg laying begins shortly afterward, usually in late May and early June. This bird is standing over its profusely marked brown eggs near Nome.

Lapland Longspur

A Lapland Longspur near Nome watches over five eggs in a cup-shaped nest made of woven grass. Thick vegetation surrounds the nest, shielding it from wind and hiding it from predators. White feathers line the cup, helping keep the eggs warm. Of the four longspur species that breed in North America, only the Lapland Longspur is not confined to the continent. The bird nests on a ribbon of treeless tundra that stretches from Scandinavia across the northern coast of Russia to the Bering Sea, and from Alaska to Quebec, Baffin Island, and western and southern Greenland.

Ovenbird

Well known for its chanting summer song and habit of hunting insects on leaf-covered forest floors, the Ovenbird is often heard but rarely seen. This photo, taken on Long Island, reveals not only the warbler, but also its distinctive nest. The female builds it in about five days without assistance from her mate, weaving together dead leaves, plant stems, bark, and pine needles and lining the inner cup with deer or horse hair. The oblong side entrance is not visible from above. The nest's resemblance to a Dutch oven gave the bird its name.

Least Grebe

Seven of the world's twenty-one grebes breed in North America. The Least Grebe, shown here, is the smallest. It has sleek, waterproof plumage, lobed toes that function like paddles when the bird pushes its feet rearward through water, and legs that are positioned far back on its body. Perfect for swimming, they make the grebe awkward on land, so the bird spends most of its life on and in the water. This Least Grebe was photographed in the Rio Grande Valley, Texas, as it settled onto its nest, a wet heap of decaying plant material surrounded by shallow water.

Green Heron

Little Blue, Snowy, and Great Egrets; Tricolored and Boat-billed Herons; Glossy Ibis; Anhinga; even grackles—Green Herons have been known to nest near all of these other colonial birds. The Green Heron nest shown here is typical: in a tree with enough branches to hide it from view and constructed from many long, thin sticks. The adult is watching over five eggs. Male and female herons share incubation duties, and since eggs that get too warm will die, both adults will stand and shade eggs from too much direct sunlight.

Black-crowned Night-Heron

Black-crowned Night-Herons can be found nesting in a variety of watery habitats from Europe to Africa, India, and Japan, and in North America from the California coast east to New Brunswick and from central Alberta and Saskatchewan south to coastal Mexico. As gregarious as it is widespread, the bird often breeds on islands, in swamps, or over water—and always in colonies, sometimes with other herons, egrets, or ibises, even Franklin's Gulls. If undisturbed, the colonies have been known to endure for as long as fifty years.

It would not be unusual to find more than a dozen Black-crowned Night-Heron nests in a single tree. Nor would it be surprising if you could look up through the bottom of the nests and see the eggs. Simple platforms made of carefully arranged two-foot-long sticks, the nests may be located on the ground or in a tree up to 160 feet high. They can be substantial or flimsy. The nest at left shelters five pale greenish blue night-heron eggs. They will hatch after twenty-three to twenty-six days of incubation by both parents. The adults will continue to adjust their stick nest while they sit.

A mane of inch-long white-tipped downy filaments covers the heads of each of the just-hatched Black-crowned Night Herons. Their eyes may be open, but the birds are nidicolous—completely dependent upon their parents and unable to leave the nest. But not for long. In only ten days, they will be strong enough to leave, and by the time they are four weeks old, they will be able to climb high above the nest. Night-herons can fly at about six weeks; they follow their parents to foraging areas shortly after that.

Least Tern

Thirteen terns in the genus *Sterna* occur in North America. Of them, the Caspian Tern is the largest. It weighs almost a pound and a half, and its spread wings measure more than four feet from tip to tip. The Least Tern, pictured here, is the smallest. It typically weighs less than two ounces, and its wingspan is only twenty inches, less than half that of the Caspian. Because the Least Tern nests on the ground, on sandy beaches along sea coasts and dried mudflats along rivers—areas that are frequently disturbed by humans—the species is endangered in California and the interior United States.

A Least Tern excavates the round depression that serves as its nest by kicking backward with its feet and rotating its body so its breast presses against all sides of the scrape. The tern below is attending a pair of speckled eggs in a nest lined with shell fragments.

Both Least Tern parents incubate. In hot weather, they will stand over their eggs to shade them. When it is very hot, they will fly low over water, letting their bellies skim the surface, and then, back at the nest, let the cool water drip onto the eggs.

The adult tern at the far left holds a fragment of the shell from which the chick in the background recently hatched. Since eggshells attract potential predators, Least Terns, like other terns, carry the pieces away from the nest shortly after hatching. If an intruder were to approach the colony despite this precaution, the highly gregarious terns would rise up to mob it as one. Single birds would dive at and defecate on the intruder, while other terns would give alarm calls. Hearing them, young on the ground would immediately find a hiding place and wait without moving until the coast is clear.

Canada Goose

Breeding Canada Geese can be found in all the lower forty-eight states and in every Canadian province, but most of the birds nest where temperatures remain chilly year-round—in Nunavit, the Northwest and Yukon territories, and Alaska. Northern-breeding geese typically arrive on territory before the snow has melted and start laying as early as mid-March. To help keep eggs and hatchlings warm under such conditions, female geese line their nests with a readily available and effective insulating material—down feathers plucked from their own breasts. These yellow and olive-green goslings were photographed in Churchill, Manitoba, shortly after they hatched.

Herring Gull

The olive-colored, speckled eggs (opposite) lying in a simple nest in Newfoundland belong to a Herring Gull. Each egg weighs between three and four ounces. Herring Gulls lay their eggs roughly two days apart, and they frequently lay three eggs, one more than is shown here. When they do, the second is often the heaviest in the clutch, while the third is the smallest. The third egg also hatches up to a day later than the other two, which hatch almost simultaneously, so the third chick starts out smaller, obtains less food, and grows more slowly than its nest mates.

The protuberance on the tip of the young Herring Gull's bill is an egg tooth. Hard, sharp-edged, and temporary, it helps chicks break out of their shells and then falls off two or three days later. Adult gulls provide no assistance as their chicks struggle out of the shells, and afterward they don't always remove the shell pieces.

Least Tern

Thirteen terns in the genus *Sterna* occur in North America. Of them, the Caspian Tern is the largest. It weighs almost a pound and a half, and its spread wings measure more than four feet from tip to tip. The Least Tern, pictured here, is the smallest. It typically weighs less than two ounces, and its wingspan is only twenty inches, less than half that of the Caspian. Because the Least Tern nests on the ground, on sandy beaches along sea coasts and dried mudflats along rivers—areas that are frequently disturbed by humans—the species is endangered in California and the interior United States.

A Least Tern excavates the round depression that serves as its nest by kicking backward with its feet and rotating its body so its breast presses against all sides of the scrape. The tern below is attending a pair of speckled eggs in a nest lined with shell fragments.

Both Least Tern parents incubate. In hot weather, they will stand over their eggs to shade them. When it is very hot, they will fly low over water, letting their bellies skim the surface, and then, back at the nest, let the cool water drip onto the eggs.

The adult tern at the far left holds a fragment of the shell from which the chick in the background recently hatched. Since eggshells attract potential predators, Least Terns, like other terns, carry the pieces away from the nest shortly after hatching. If an intruder were to approach the colony despite this precaution, the highly gregarious terns would rise up to mob it as one. Single birds would dive at and defecate on the intruder, while other terns would give alarm calls. Hearing them, young on the ground would immediately find a hiding place and wait without moving until the coast is clear.

Breeding Canada Geese can be found in all the lower forty-eight states and in every Canadian province, but most of the birds nest where temperatures remain chilly year-round—in Nunavit, the Northwest and Yukon territories, and Alaska. Northern-breeding geese typically arrive on territory before the snow has melted and start laying as early as mid-March. To help keep eggs and hatchlings warm under such conditions, female geese line their nests with a readily available and effective insulating material—down feathers plucked from their own breasts. These yellow and olive-green goslings were photographed in Churchill, Manitoba, shortly after they hatched.

Herring Gull

The olive-colored, speckled eggs (opposite) lying in a simple nest in Newfoundland belong to a Herring Gull. Each egg weighs between three and four ounces. Herring Gulls lay their eggs roughly two days apart, and they frequently lay three eggs, one more than is shown here. When they do, the second is often the heaviest in the clutch, while the third is the smallest. The third egg also hatches up to a day later than the other two, which hatch almost simultaneously, so the third chick starts out smaller, obtains less food, and grows more slowly than its nest mates.

The protuberance on the tip of the young Herring Gull's bill is an egg tooth. Hard, sharp-edged, and temporary, it helps chicks break out of their shells and then falls off two or three days later. Adult gulls provide no assistance as their chicks struggle out of the shells, and afterward they don't always remove the shell pieces.

ALTHOUGH IT'S TRUE THAT cassowaries, emus, and other birds are unable to fly, and that a few birds, such as the Wood Duck, lose the ability to fly for a short time each year while they molt, the vast majority of the world's adult birds do fly—and for good reason: Their lives depend upon it.

Picture a songbird that suddenly lost the ability to fly. Lacking the great size and the foot speed of the ostrich, perhaps the most famous of the world's flightless species, it would no longer be able to elude its predators, and its ability to gather food would vanish. Vulnerable and at risk of starving, it would act less like a capable adult and more like a just-hatched chick.

Ornithologists categorize chicks on the basis of how developed they are at hatching: Those that lack feathers and are utterly dependent upon their parents are called altricial, while those that appear with a thick coat of down and are independent enough to leave the nest are known as precocial.

Whether a chick is altricial or precocial varies from species to species. Young of both types have enormous amounts of growing and developing to do before they can fly, and both benefit from the remarkable ways that nature has taught adult birds to protect and feed them.

Northern Mockingbird

Northern Mockingbirds typically leave the nest when they are twelve to fourteen days old. When they go, their weight will be ten times what it was when they hatched, and even so, it will be only sixty to seventy percent of what they will weigh as an adult. The fuel for their rapid growth will be primarily spiders and insects and, later, fruit—and all of it will come from the parents. Delivering only one food item at a time, adult mockingbirds will make up to five deliveries per hour per nestling, and the male will continue to feed the young for up to three weeks after they fledge.

Barn Swallow

Long-winged and fork-tailed, Barn Swallows are a pleasure to watch as they hunt insects. The birds dip and climb and veer left and right with great ease, and they are conscientious providers, returning to the nest an average of twenty-nine times an hour to feed their young. Both parents do the feeding, and if they bring off two broods, juveniles from the first may help feed their siblings in the second. Barn Swallows usually feed only one chick each time they return to the nest. The nestling that opens its mouth the widest and reaches forward the farthest gets the food.

Four recently hatched Barn Swallow chicks crowd together in this nest in southeastern Arizona. Like Cliff Swallows, Barn Swallows fashion their nests out of mud pellets, but they appear to prefer nesting individually, not in a colony, and their nests are cup-shaped, not enclosed. Long ago Barn Swallows nested primarily in caves. Now they rear their young almost exclusively on and in man-made structures. Sheds, barns, garages, bridges, culverts . . . almost any sort of building will do, so long as there is a ledge or vertical surface to build on and a horizontal surface overhead to provide shelter.

Barn Swallows typically lay clutches containing four or five eggs, which hatch after thirteen to seventeen days of incubation,

mostly by the female. The hatchlings' bills appear cream-colored on the outside but are a striking yellow-orange on the inside, and their open mouths are rimmed with an even brighter whitish yellow. For parents looking to feed hungry chicks, the gaping bills make targets that are hard to miss, even when the light is dim. Pin feathers visible on the swallows' breasts indicate that these birds hatched at least eight days ago.

Black-and-white Warbler

The Black-and-white Warbler, which spends the winter in south-eastern states, throughout the West Indies, and from Mexico south to Colombia and western Venezuela, is one of the earliest warblers to return to its breeding grounds each spring. Seen regularly along the Gulf coast the second week of March, it arrives in the Midwest and mid-Atlantic states by early April. In New York, where this photo was taken, the bird lays its eggs as early as the second week of May. Its nest is a well-hidden cup about four inches in diameter located at the foot of a tree or shrub.

Western Sandpiper

Temperatures during the breeding season range from 45 degrees F to 59 degrees between the Yukon and Kuskokwim Rivers in Alaska, in the southern portion of the Western Sandpiper's breeding area. They can fall below freezing around Point Barrow, five hundred miles to the north, at the limit of the sandpiper's range. Adult birds nesting between these locations have to cover their young with their wings to keep them warm at night and when it rains. This Western Sandpiper in Nome was photographed as its spotted white breast feathers were being ruffled by a heat-seeking hatchling.

Pied-billed Grebe

Feathers play an important role in the diet of the Pied-billed Grebe. Most grebes eat large quantities of their own feathers; they also feed them to newly hatched young. Scientists believe the feathers keep the sharp parts of fish, crustaceans, and other prey items from piercing the bird's stomach and passing from the stomach into the small intestines before they are dissolved. Swallowed feathers are also thought to help the birds form pellets.

Long-billed Curlew

Nests constructed by Long-billed Curlews are little more than lined, shallow depressions in the ground, so they and their occupants are vulnerable to raids by hungry coyotes, foxes, badgers, and snakes. Adult curlews will vigorously chase and attack potential nest predators, and they are equally watchful for Swainson's and Ferruginous Hawks and corvids. This photo was taken in Teton Valley, Idaho, as an adult Long-billed Curlew circled its own nest in great agitation, screaming and diving at an approaching Black-billed Magpie.

White-tailed Hawk

The White-tailed Hawk typically builds its nests in the tops of dense, thorny shrubs or cacti—locations that are difficult for snakes, skunks, raccoons, and other ground predators to reach. But the bird still faces avian challengers. Both the Crested Caracara and Great Horned Owl find the hawk's two- or three-foot-wide platform of branches, twigs, and grasses to their liking. The caracara claims old nests, but the owl may usurp active nests. Both have been known to kill nestlings. The pair of dark-eyed hawk chicks at left are awaiting the return of a parent.

The White-tailed Hawk frequently hunts from perches, but it also snatches flying insects out of mid-air and searches for prey on the ground while hanging motionless overhead on outstretched wings in a strong breeze. Both parents bring food to their offspring. The young hawks are able to fly when they leave the nest at about seven weeks of age, but they rely on their parents for food for as long as seven months.

Crested Caracara

Though known as a carrion feeder, the Crested Caracara is actually an opportunistic forager that consumes any animal dead or alive, commonly steals food from other birds, including White-tailed Hawks, and may in fact be more interested in the insects that crawl and fly around carrion than in the dead animal itself. Adult caracaras feed their young more live-caught prey than carrion, tearing the prey into pieces before delivering it.

Both male and female adult caracaras gather the vine pieces, weed stalks, twigs, and other material they use to construct their shallow, bowl-shaped nests. Both sexes also incubate the eggs and bring food to hatchlings. Thick natal down covers these three caracara chicks, the dark brown on their shoulders, foreheads, and crowns hinting at the adult plumage to come later.

Food eaten by a bird passes through its esophagus to the stomach, but it doesn't go there directly. In many species, including Crested Caracaras, the food is stored first in a saclike enlargement of the esophagus known as the crop. In addition to softening the food and regulating its movement through the digestive system, the crop enables birds to gather food in one place and digest it in another. That the chicks at right have just eaten is obvious; their crops are swollen with food and protrude conspicuously from beneath the tracts of feathers that ordinarily cover them.

Great Crested Flycatcher

The Great Crested Flycatcher is one of thirty-seven tyrant flycatchers that breed in North America. Like wood-pewees, phoebes, kingbirds, and other relatives, it is well known for the way it hunts: From a perch, it waits for an insect to fly past. When one does, the bird flies out, snatches the insect out of mid-air, then returns to the perch. The Great Crested, a near double of the Dusky-capped, Ash-throated, and Brown-crested Flycatchers of the Southwest, is the only cavity-nesting flycatcher in the eastern half of the continent. This one had a nest in the Adirondack Mountains.

Golden-fronted Woodpecker

The Golden-fronted Woodpecker, like all woodpeckers, feeds on an assortment of insects, but its bill is pointed and slightly curved, not chisel-tipped and straight, so the bird doesn't do the extensive drilling and hammering typical of other foraging woodpeckers. Instead, it fly-catches, probes crevices and holes using its tongue, and gleans and taps. Like the Lewis's, Red-headed, Acorn, Gila, and Red-bellied Woodpeckers, it also consumes nuts, fruits, and seeds. This red-crowned male was photographed as it returned to its nest with berries from a lotebush.

Bewick's Wren

This dusty brown Bewick's Wren has had a successful hunt. No doubt a nest cavity is a short flight away, and inside it at least one hungry chick is waiting. A female wren may accompany her mate on hunting trips while she is laying, but as soon as her three- to eight-egg clutch is complete, she starts incubating. While she broods, the male forages not just for himself but for her as well. Both parents will gather food for the young after the eggs hatch, in about two weeks, but the female may be the only one who feeds the chicks.

Great Kiskadee

The Great Kiskadee is a master of sallying out from a perch to capture insects in mid air, but it eats far more than arthropods, and it has more strategies for obtaining food than any other flycatcher. Versatile and omnivorous, the kiskadee has been observed gleaning, hovering like a kingfisher, plunging from a perch, and wading. It readily consumes fruit, snails, tadpoles, small snakes, fish as big as three inches long, even lizards. It also likes dog food.

Broad-billed Hummingbird

Among hummingbirds, the job of caring for the young falls entirely to the female; after mating, the male hummingbird has nothing to do with its offspring. The female alone incubates and feeds the nestlings. The shimmering female Broad-billed Hummingbird shown here is regurgitating food directly into the throat of one of the two chicks huddling in the nest. Hummingbirds are known for lapping nectar from flowers, but a hatchling's diet is typically all insects. Nectar is added to the diet after two weeks.

Eastern Bluebird

It is the female Eastern Bluebird that builds the nest and incubates the eggs, but the male and female together feed the hatchlings. At right, a begging chick meets its parent at the entrance to a nest in a naturally occurring tree cavity. Bluebirds will also nest in holes created by woodpeckers, and they readily take to nest boxes.

Hatchlings typically leave the nest seventeen to nineteen days after hatching. Their parents will continue to bring them butterfly and moth larvae, spiders, grasshoppers, and crickets for another three weeks after they fledge.

Western Screech-Owl

Three screech-owls breed in North America: the tiny
Whiskered Screech-Owl, which occurs in the United States
only in southeastern Arizona, and the nearly identical
Eastern and Western Screech-Owls. The Eastern can be
found from the Great Plains states east, while the Western
Screech-Owl, shown here, nests along the Pacific coast
from southeastern Alaska to central Mexico and as far east
as Colorado. Screech-owls rely on their streaked and barred
plumage to blend in with their surroundings while roosting
during the day. They use their excellent vision while hunting
at night. The owl at left has caught a banded gecko, a
species seldom seen during the day.

Pileated Woodpeckers and Northern and Gilded Flickers
are unwitting friends of the Western Screech-Owl—the
cavities they excavate in trees often become screech-owl
nests. The seven- to ten-inch-long, five-ounce owl lays its
eggs in a wide variety of sites: in nest boxes; in fir-dominated
forests; in river-fringing stands of cottonwood, tamarisk,
and willow; in saguaro cacti and Joshua trees; and, like the
owl at right, in bosques of mesquite. The bird is standing in
an entrance hole that is barely larger than the diameter of
its own body.

Atlantic Puffin

Backward-pointing spines on its tongue and the roof of its mouth enable the Atlantic Puffin to hunt fish even as it holds the prey it's already caught. The bird forages underwater. Flapping its wings to propel itself as far as two hundred feet below the surface and using its webbed feet as rudders, it can catch and hold dozens of fish at the same time. This puffin on Machias Seal Island, Maine, has just returned from a successful foraging trip. Clenched between its mandibles are several slender capelin, which the puffin will deliver to a chick waiting in a nearby nest burrow.

Common Tern

Foraging Common Terns do not sit on the water and dive after fish. Instead, they fly low over the water and, facing into the wind, hold their positions as they look for prey. Spotting a school of fish, they swoop down and either pick them from the surface or, folding their wings, shoot into the water like an arrow. The terns in this photo are working to become airborne after plunge-diving. Two of the birds have caught fish. The third wasn't as lucky; its empty bill is poking through the wing feathers of the bird just ahead of it.

American White Pelican

Unlike the Brown Pelican, the American White Pelican does not make spectacular plunge-dives from the air while foraging. Instead, it hunts as it swims, dipping its lengthy bill into the water to scoop fish into the pouch in its lower mandible. The white pelican often forages cooperatively with other pelicans, but the bird shown here wasn't about to work that hard for a meal—the photo was taken off the coast of Florida just after the pelican landed near fishermen who were discarding fish scraps from a boat.

Great Egret

Droplets glisten in the sunlight an instant after the foraging Great Egret at left thrust its bill into the water and quickly pulled it out again. Wading egrets will occasionally move their feet in an attempt to scare submerged prey out of their hiding places, but most birds prefer simply to stand patiently and watch what swims by. A tiny fish, a tasty reward for this hunter's patience and diligence, wriggles in the egret's bill.

The egret at right is feeding on fish that a receding tide has stranded in a dark lagoon. Bright sunlight illuminates the bird from behind, revealing in startling X-ray-like fashion just how much of the egret is feathers and how little is flesh and bone. Each feather of the bird's fanned tail and spread wings glows bright white in the light, and it is easy to see how much one feather overlaps another. Orderly rows of short feathers called coverts line the underside of each wing.

Cactus Wren

Of the nine species of wrens that breed in North America, the Cactus Wren inhabits the most forbidding habitat: the scorching deserts of southern California, southern Nevada, Arizona, New Mexico, Texas, and northern and central Mexico. Although the wren has been observed drinking from an opening in a saguaro cactus made by a Gila Woodpecker, eating the juicy pulp of saguaro fruit, and visiting backyard birdbaths, most of the water the bird needs to survive comes from the insects, spiders, and occasional small lizards that are its prey.

Curve-billed Thrasher

Common names of birds can be confusing. Of the seven thrashers that breed in southwestern North America, the California, Crissal, and Le Conte's Thrashers all have bills that curve downward more than that of the Curve-billed Thrasher, but this species was discovered and named first. It occurs year-round from the California-Arizona border to the Oklahoma panhandle, across much of Texas, and south to Oaxaca in Mexico. This bird in Green Valley, south of Tucson, tends two chicks in a nest of twigs in a prickly cholla cactus.

Black-throated Sparrow

The migratory movements of the Black-throated
Sparrow are as nuanced as the bird is beautiful.
The species can be found year-round from southern
Arizona, southern New Mexico, and central Texas
south to Baja California and central Mexico, but
populations also breed in southwestern Oregon
and southern Idaho and as far north as Washington
east of the Cascades. So each spring and fall, some
birds migrate long distances, some migrate short
distances within their breeding ranges, and others
move only up to or down from high-elevation
nesting areas. Like all sparrows, the black-throat
supplements its diet of seeds and grasses with
insects during the breeding season.

Ferruginous
Pygmy-Owl

Barely seven inches from head to tail
and weighing only a little more than
two ounces, the fast-flying Ferruginous
Pygmy-Owl is nonetheless a bold hunter.
Active in the daytime and early evening,
it consumes an assortment of insects,
reptiles, amphibians, birds, and small
mammals. This bird in Altar Valley,
Arizona, eats a cicada in a cavity in a
saguaro. Like the closely related Northern
Pygmy-Owl, the only other pygmy-owl
that breeds in the United States, the
Ferruginous Pygmy-Owl has a pair of
dark spots on the back of its head that
look like backward-peering eyes.

Northern
Harrier

Most hawks search for prey from a high perch or while soaring, but harriers are different. They hunt more like Barn Owls and Long-eared and Short-eared Owls. Gliding buoyantly over prairies, marshes, and other open habitats, rarely more than ten or fifteen feet above the ground, harriers use owl-like circular ear funnels on each side of their faces to zero in on the sounds of rodents, birds, reptiles, and frogs below. This female Northern Harrier is plucking a just-caught bird. The upperparts of male Northern Harriers are not brown but silvery gray.

Wilson's Phalarope

Phalaropes are members of the sandpiper family, but they feed in a manner quite unlike their relatives. Sandpipers forage while standing, feeding on tiny creatures they locate by sight or by probing in mud or sand. This Wilson's Phalarope is foraging while swimming, picking items off the water's surface at the Bear River refuge in Utah. Like Red and Red-necked Phalaropes, Wilson's is well known for hunting by swimming in a tight circle, creating a rotating column of water that lifts prey toward the surface, but the bird won't spin if more easily obtainable prey is abundant.

Mountain Bluebird

Many of the colors of birds are produced by pigments in their feathers. Melanins are responsible for blacks, browns, and pale yellows. Carotenoids create reds, orange, and other yellows. And porphyrins produce bright browns, magenta, and parrot green. No pigment, however, is responsible for the brilliant blue of this Mountain Bluebird. Like the indigo of Indigo Buntings and the blue of Blue Jays, it is a structural color, created when particles on the surface of each feather barb scatter the shortest wavelengths of the light that strikes them.

Marsh Wren

Male Marsh Wrens build many nests each spring, weaving grasses, sedges, and cattails into complicated domed structures like this one. Prospective mates tour the nests and either accept one, which they subsequently line with cattail down, rootlets, and other materials, or begin building a new nest. Only the female Marsh Wren incubates the eggs and broods the hatchlings, two of which can be seen in this photo. They're holding their bills open wide, revealing bright red targets for their parent, which will place insects and spiders into them.

Belted Kingfisher

This Belted Kingfisher was photographed soon after it had dived into the water and returned to its perch with a fish. The long-billed bird looks more like an angler than an earth mover. Yet the Belted Kingfisher, like the Green and Ringed Kingfishers, the only other members of the family Alcedinidae that breed in North America, lays its eggs and rears its young underground, in a chamber located at the end of a three- to six-foot-long tunnel the bird excavates in an earthen bank. The bird shoots a plume of dirt out the tunnel's entrance as it digs.

Yellow-crowned Night-Heron

Unlike the Black-crowned Night-Heron, which eats a variety of prey, including tern eggs and chicks, the methodical Yellow-crowned Night-Heron specializes. In lowlands and coastal areas primarily in the deep south, it stalks only one prey: crabs. While foraging, it typically stands and waits. Then it walks slowly. Then it stands again. When it finally spots a crab, it lunges. The bird will swallow small crustaceans whole, but it will shake a large crab repeatedly until all of its legs and pincers have broken off. Then the night-heron will either use its bill to crush the body into bite-size morsels, or perhaps eat the now-smaller prey whole.

Wading slowly or crouching patiently on rocks or branches near water, the Green Heron hunts a wide range of prey. A well-known consumer of snakes, toads, frogs, and especially fish, the bird also hunts dragonflies, grasshoppers, crickets, crayfish, crabs, and snails, as well as leeches and earthworms. One of only a few birds that use tools, Green Herons will drop mayflies, feathers, and other bait into the water and then strike at the fish that come to investigate.

Elf Owl

The Elf Owl is the smallest of the nineteen owls that occur in North America, and perhaps the most abundant raptor in the upland deserts of Arizona and Sonora, Mexico. The owl above, photographed in Madera Canyon, enters its nest cavity following a successful foraging trip. Elf Owls eat mostly insects and hunt only at dusk and at night; they are occasionally seen swooping near campfires, lighted windows, and outdoor lights. The birds are present in Arizona from March or April through September and spend the winter in central and southern Mexico.

The Elf Owl often nests in holes in utility poles and fence posts made by Acorn and Ladder-backed Woodpeckers. It will also occupy nest boxes, but all known natural nest sites in Texas, southwestern New Mexico, southern Arizona, and Sonora are in holes that woodpeckers have excavated in saguaros, cottonwoods, willows, sycamores, and other trees. Many of the entrances to the cavities are less than three inches in diameter—just right for an owl that is shy of six inches long and weighs less than two ounces.

Aplomado Falcon

The band on the right leg of this Aplomado Falcon is an indicator of its special status. Fairly common at the beginning of the twentieth century on the grasslands of the Southwest, where it fed on Horned Larks, Brewer's Sparrows, and other birds, as well as small rodents and insects, the bird had all but disappeared by 1930. The northern subspecies has been on the federal endangered species list since 1986. As all raptors do, this falcon carries its prey to an area shielded from the view of other birds.

Greater Roadrunner

The changing seasons dictate the diet of the Greater Roadrunner. In summer, insects are preferred because they are abundant, but during the breeding season, when chicks are in the nest, roadrunners hunt lizards, snakes, mice, and other vertebrates. In winter, when cold weather makes insects, spiders, and reptiles less available, roadrunners switch again, this time to seeds and fruits, and to other birds: Roadrunners eat bird eggs and young, regularly lie in wait at feeders and birdhouses, and have been known to leap from the ground to knock down hummingbirds and White-throated Swifts.

Common Nighthawk

Common Nighthawks, like flycatchers, hunt flying insects. But nighthawks do not sit on a perch waiting for prey to happen by. Instead, they fly continuously, sometimes in flocks containing hundreds of birds. When they come upon queen ants, beetles, and other airborne insect prey, they seize them in their short, wide bills. The birds typically forage at dusk and dawn, starting about half an hour before sunset and again an hour before sunrise. They frequently gather around insect swarms attracted to artificial lighting. This bird is dipping low with its mouth open, grabbing a drink on the fly.

Black-necked Stilt

The graphic black and white plumage and long pink legs of the Black-necked Stilt are unique among the birds of North America. This stilt is bending its leg at what appears to be a knee, but its real knees are above, hidden from view by white belly feathers. The backward-flexing joint is actually the equivalent of our ankle. Above it is the tibiotarsus, the equivalent of our shin. The tarsometatarsus, or instep, is below. Like all birds, the stilt walks on its toes.

Great Egret

Great Egrets eat mainly small fish, but they also hunt crayfish, prawns, shrimp, and other invertebrates as well as frogs, tadpoles, lizards, snakes, and small mammals. This egret has just caught a frog, which it is holding crosswise in its bill. It will rotate the frog by quickly opening and closing its mandibles while moving its head, until the frog points down the bird's throat. Then the egret will swallow it whole.

Broad-billed Hummingbird

This Broad-billed Hummingbird nest consists of shreds of bark, grasses, bits of leaves, and spider silk. It is lined with white plant down and has been molded to match the body shape of the female that built it. Only about one inch tall and three-quarters of an inch wide, it is home for two young hummingbirds about fifteen to twenty days old, but they are rapidly outgrowing it. In less than a week, both birds will leave the tiny nest for good.

Ornithologists have documented a close association between the length and shape of a hummingbird's bill and the dimensions of the flowers on which the bird feeds. This Green Hermit's distinctly decurved bill enables it to reach deep inside long, tube-shaped flowers. Because such resources are widely dispersed in the tropics, the hermit pursues a feeding strategy known as trap-lining—it regularly flies from flower to flower, following the same route each day.

The Black-chinned Hummingbird consumes insects, gleaning them from the surface of plants, snatching them out of mid-air, even picking them off spiderwebs. It will also lap up sap oozing from holes drilled in trees by sapsuckers and drink sugar water from feeders. The bird in this photo is hovering near a red blossom on cane cholla, one of the ninety species of plants from which it takes nectar.

Barn Owl

Barn Owls have excellent vision, and they can locate voles, cotton rats, shrews, and other small mammals by sound alone with astonishing accuracy. The birds seize such prey using their feet, then bite through the animal's skull. The male does all the hunting while his mate incubates and broods the hatchlings, but the female does the actual feeding. Until her young can swallow a mouse whole, she dutifully tears apart each food item and places the pieces into her owlets' mouths. By the time the birds are as large as these owls, both parents simply drop the prey in the nest and resume hunting.

Gila
Woodpecker

The brown-headed female Gila Woodpecker at left is carrying an insect back to its nest cavity. Her mate, identifiable as a male by the red feathers on its head, peers out from inside. Breeding Gila Woodpeckers share incubation and feeding duties, and both parents help excavate their nest cavity. When the nest site is a saguaro, as it is here, several months can pass between excavation and occupation. That's because a cactus is wet inside. When its outer layer is breached, it exudes a protective fluid that coats the cavity. In time the secretion hardens, forming a dry shell.

The Gila Woodpecker eats primarily beetles, moths, cicadas, and other insects, but like all woodpeckers, it isn't known for being choosy. It has been observed eating earthworms, small lizards, and the eggs and young of wood-warblers, vireos, tanagers, and other birds, as well as bacon rinds. And it has a sweet tooth, which leads it to consume fruits and berries, even to drink sugar water from hummingbird feeders. Above, a red-crowned male eats pollen from a flower on a saguaro. The plant will later produce a figlike fruit that the woodpecker also likes to eat.

Northern Gannet

A Northern Gannet pair produces only one egg each season, as early as the end of April or as late as mid-June. It hatches in about six weeks. In no time, the chick looks like the nestlings in this photo. Brooding and feeding responsibilities fill the parents' next twelve weeks. Then the chick makes its first "flight." Flinging itself from a cliff, it drops swiftly to the water below. Then, either because it is too fat and its wings are too small or because it still lacks the muscle power to lift itself from the water, the fledgling starts its first southward migration—not by flying, but by swimming.

Imperial Shag

Most Imperial Shag clutches consist of three eggs. Both adults take turns keeping the eggs warm by cradling them on the webs of their feet. The pair splits responsibility for caring for the hatchlings as well. Field researchers in Antarctica have observed that male shags typically attend the nest from midnight to noon and then leave to forage for food in the afternoon. Females do just the opposite: They forage in the morning and return to care for the young as their mate departs. This adult is holding its bill open so its tiny chick can receive a regurgitated meal.

Cooper's Hawk

Chipmunks, rodents, and medium-size birds such as robins, jays, flickers, and starlings are the principal prey of the Cooper's Hawk, one of three species in the genus *Accipiter* that breed in North America. Only the tip of a dead bird's outstretched wing is visible here. This Cooper's Hawk has no intention of allowing another bird to steal its meal, so it is fanning its tail and spreading it wings to shield the prey from view.

Prairie Falcon

The bird lying limp at the feet of this Prairie Falcon is a Gambel's Quail. It and other birds—Horned Larks, Lark Buntings, meadow larks, Lapland Longspurs—make up an important part of the falcon's diet when ground squirrels, its principal prey, retreat to their burrows in June and July. The Prairie Falcon breeds as far east as western Nebraska and western North and South Dakota, as far west as California and the east side of the Cascades in Oregon and Washington, and as far south as San Luis Potosi in Mexico—and it wanders widely after breeding.

Scientists estimate that there are more than one hundred thousand breeding pairs of Brown Pelicans in the world today, enough to make this scene a familiar sight in much of the coastal United States. That the total is so healthy is significant, because as recently as 1970, after nearly every North American population had vanished, the Brown Pelican was placed on the federal endangered species list. Synthetic pesticides including DDT were shown to be the cause of the bird's decline. After their use was curtailed or banned outright, reproduction rates improved, and the pelican, and other birds, came back.

The higher a pelican is when it starts its plunge, the greater its airspeed will be as it dives, and the deeper it will be able to penetrate into the water. The Brown Pelican below, photographed at Puerto Penasco, Mexico, has spotted a fish and is hurtling toward it head-first. As the bird dives, it pulls its legs forward and bends its wings, pointing the long, black wingtips toward the sky. The instant the pelican enters the water, it will push its legs and wings backward, thrusting the bill, with its quickly expanding pouch, toward the fish.

Bald Eagle

"No sooner does the Fish Hawk make its appearance along our Atlantic shores, or ascend our numerous and large rivers, than the Eagle follows it, and, like a selfish oppressor, robs it of the hard-earned fruits of its labour." That's how Audubon described the Bald Eagle's penchant for taking fish from Ospreys. The eagle steals from other eagles, too, and it prefers eating carrion over hunting for itself. But this photo, taken on Alaska's Kenai Peninsula, shows that it will hunt when it has to. Fish are common prey, as are many species of birds.

Great Blue Heron

Newly hatched Great Blue Heron chicks weigh less than two ounces and are covered with pale gray down. Their wings are mostly unfeathered. Both adults provide for the nestlings, placing food directly into their mouths or regurgitating into the nest, and growth is rapid: The chicks can stand at fourteen days and walk steadily at twenty-one days. Wing flapping begins in the fourth week. Young great blues fly from the nest when they are seven to eight weeks old but return to be fed by adults for another three weeks.

Common Tern

Little more than a handful of sea grass laid across a shallow scrape in the sand, this Common Tern's nest could hardly look less impressive. Yet it is just right for this adult and recently hatched chick—it is close to vegetation in which the chick could find shelter, if necessary, and only a short flight from the sea, where the parents find food. Most tern nests sit above the highest point reached by the tide.

Common Black-Hawk

The Common Black-Hawk, a year-round resident of Central
America and northwestern South America, is only a summer
visitor to the United States. It can be found in central Arizona,
southwest New Mexico, and west Texas from March or early April
until October, but only in small numbers. The Texas population,
located in Jeff Davis County, consists of about ten pairs; only 200
to 250 pairs make up the entire U.S. breeding population, the
majority in Arizona. This crowded nest is in Aravaipa Canyon,
north of Tucson. Nestlings can be seen jostling for space below
the adult on the rim.

Elegant Trogon

The red ring around the eye, yellow bill, and metallic green sheen on the black head of this male Elegant Trogon give only a hint of the bird's colorful appearance. It also sports a bright red chest and belly, gray upper wings, and iridescent copper-green tail feathers. The bird was photographed in a typical nest site: a hole in a sycamore tree that was excavated by a Northern Flicker. Male trogons attempting to persuade a mate to accept a nest cavity will often perch near it, or even in it, and call continuously.

Great Gray Owl

The line dividing the nesting duties of the male from those of the female is sharply drawn for Great Gray Owls. Only the female incubates the eggs and broods the young, and she alone gives food to the owlets. Throughout the four to five weeks the female sits on her eggs, the male does all the hunting, returning with small prey for the female about once every four hours. Male great grays continue to provide food not only after hatching but for the next three months as well, long after the owlets have left the nest and begun to fly and the female has abandoned them.

FINDING NOURISHMENT efficiently is mandatory for all living creatures. The benefit gained from the food they eat must exceed the cost, measured in time and effort, of acquiring it.

The imperative places an extraordinary burden on birds, many of which live in environments where suitable prey isn't easily come by. For albatrosses, terns, skimmers, penguins, and other piscivorous birds, efficient foraging means detecting prey while flying over or swimming in often vast bodies of water—and then seizing it without drowning. For hawks, falcons, owls, and other carnivores, it means executing well-aimed, perfectly timed strikes. And for insectivores such as nighthawks and flycatchers, it means not just flying, but snatching insects out of mid-air.

Dramatic growth and development must take place before a chick can make its first flight, much less master these specialized hunting techniques. Soft, fluffy down feathers must be replaced with firm-vaned flight feathers; wings and tails have to extend to full size; and muscles must grow strong enough to power flight. And, of course, the near-adult bird must have an opportunity to perfect its flying and hunting. That birds are able to accomplish all this in the tiny window of time between spring and autumn is an accomplishment to rival flight itself.

Least Tern

Unlike pelicans, pigeons, hummingbirds, woodpeckers, and an assortment of other altricial birds, which are featherless, helpless, and utterly dependent upon their parents immediately after hatching, Least Terns emerge from the shell with open eyes and a complete coat of down—and they leave the nest within two days. Despite their peregrinations, the hatchlings above stayed still long enough for their parents to feed them. The adults deliver as many as two fish every hour, and continue to feed the youngsters even after they make their first flight, when they are about twenty days old.

Least Terns seen in North America, northern Mexico, or the Caribbean beginning in late March and April depart these areas entirely in late summer or early fall. They fly well south and spend the winter along the Pacific coast of southern Mexico and the east coasts of Mexico and Central and South America. For six to eight weeks before they go, however, adults and fledglings like the one at left come together from many nests to feed, loaf, and roost on their coastal breeding grounds.

American Redstart

When any chick leaves the nest, it almost always enters a less comfortable and more dangerous world. Removed from its parents, which once sheltered it from sun, rain, and cold, the young bird is exposed to harsh weather. Unable to fly, at least for a short time, it may also be unable to escape from predators. When the American Redstart at right fledged, its wings and tail were only about half grown. It flew clumsily but needed only a day or so before it could join its parents in the canopy above.

Young redstarts ordinarily depend on their parents for most of their food during their first week out of the nest, and their parents continue to bring them plant-hoppers, flies, wasps, and other insects for up to three weeks. But redstart parents divvy up the brood, so one feeds some fledglings while the other sees to the rest. The gray head and bright yellow patches on the outer tail feathers indicate that the adult below is a female. Male American Redstarts have black heads and bright orange markings.

Canada Goose

Arctic and red foxes; Herring, Iceland, Glaucous-winged, and Glaucous Gulls; and Parasitic and Long-tailed Jaegers all eat Canada Goose eggs, and the foxes and gulls are a threat to goslings, too, as are Bald Eagles. Both adult geese defend the nest against such predators, but this duty falls primarily to the male when the female is incubating. The adult below appears to realize that exposure to the elements can also be a cause of mortality among goslings. It is sheltering a chick in its back feathers, which the goose has puffed up to increase the amount of heat they trap.

Goslings can walk within hours of hatching. After a day, they will be able to swim and dive. In fact, parents usually lead their young away from the nest within the first twenty-four hours of their lives. Contour feathers will begin to emerge on the chicks' wings and tails by the end of their third week, and the species' characteristic black neck and head and white cheeks will appear in week seven. By the end of the following week, the metamorphosis from golden puffball to brownish goose will be complete, and the two-month-old bird will make its first flight.

Black Skimmer

Herring and Laughing Gulls are at the top of the list of predators that eat the eggs and young of the Black Skimmer. Here, an adult skimmer gingerly picks up its tiny chick to move it to safety as a flock of gulls harasses the pair from above. The only species of its genus to breed in North America, the Black Skimmer can be found along the Pacific coast in San Diego and Orange Counties in California and along the Gulf and Atlantic coasts as far north as Massachusetts and Long Island.

Least Grebe

Least Grebes frequently swim with their young on their backs, but the chicks aren't afraid of the water; they can swim and dive soon after hatching. And it's a good thing they can, because Least Grebe families typically leave the nest as soon as the last of their eggs has hatched. The black-and-white-striped chicks spend their first three or four days between one parent's wings while the other adult forages. The young birds are able to climb there as soon as twenty minutes after hatching. Within forty minutes, the parent may dive with the young aboard.

One of the principal threats to a young Least Grebe is another grebe. During nesting season, Pied-billed Grebes may chase Least Grebes from their territories. On small bodies of water, they have been known to attack and kill Least Grebe chicks. Faced with such a threat, the smaller bird will typically dive and hide by allowing only its head or the tip of its bill to break the surface of the water.

The fuzzy-headed young Barn Owl below rests amid yellow flowers in Texas—in broad daylight. A dense coat of long, grayish white down covers the bird's head and back, but spotted ochre-colored adult feathers are already visible on the wings, and more are on the way elsewhere on its body. The owl is molting into its basic plumage. By the time it reaches eight or nine weeks of age, a developmental landmark probably no more than a couple weeks away, it will be essentially indistinguishable from its parents and ready to fledge.

The Barn Owl at right is nearly ready to make its first flight. Its prebasic molt is complete; the coat of fuzzy down the bird wore after hatching has been replaced by the patterned feathers of an adult. Barn Owls usually depart their nest about eight or nine weeks after hatching, but they have much to learn about flying and hunting when they go. As they perfect their skills over the next three to five weeks, they remain dependent upon their parents for food. Then, finally able to feed themselves, the young owls disperse.

Masked Booby

Masked Boobies lay one or two eggs, never three, and on average only about sixty percent of booby eggs hatch, so it isn't unusual to count only one hatchling per nest. Also to be expected is that siblicide may have played a role in the count. In nests where two eggs do hatch, the first may hatch as many as ten days before the second. Much bigger and stronger than the second hatchling, the first chick typically forces its sibling out of the nest. Unprotected by the parents, the ejected bird usually dies of exposure and is quickly scavenged by land birds, frigatebirds, and crabs.

Wandering Albatross

Like all albatrosses, the Wandering Albatross devotes a huge amount of time to caring for its young. Every other year between mid-December and mid-January (summer in the Southern Hemisphere), it lays one egg, which hatches after seventy-seven or seventy-eight days of incubation. The parents keep the hatchling warm for another month, but they feed it for about a year; 278 days after hatching, the young bird finally departs for the sea. Most Wandering Albatrosses will not return to nest on land until they are five, six, or even seven years old.

Common Tern

Incubating Common Terns take care not to leave a predator-attracting stain of whitewash anywhere near their eggs; they always fly from the nest before defecating. And they are just as careful after the eggs hatch. Within fifteen minutes, a parent will fly off with the eggshell pieces and drop them far from the nest. The days-old chick pictured below is demonstrating perhaps the tern's best defense against predators: Able to stand within hours of hatching, it left the nest shortly after its feathers dried, thus preventing a predator from discovering and eating it and its siblings all at once.

Dark tips on the gray feathers of the back, a black bar above the bend of the wing, and a bill that is mostly black, not the brilliant orange red of an adult—all are characteristics of a Common Tern that has fully replaced its downy covering with true feathers but is not yet one year old. Juvenile terns practice hunting over water within days of fledging and accompany their parents to the feeding grounds after a week or so, but they will not catch fish for themselves for at least another ten days.

Western Sandpiper

White and buffy down covers the underside of this Western Sandpiper, a dark wavy stripe passes over each eye, and reddish brown blotches mark its back, wings, and thighs. The granular-looking white dots visible on the peep's upperparts are actually the white tips of dark brown down filaments. Western Sandpipers leave the nest within twenty-four hours of hatching. Both parents accompany and protect the chicks but abandon them once they can fly, about three weeks after hatching, and the adults usually leave the breeding ground before their offspring.

The quartet of young Burrowing Owls below was photographed near Tucson. Able to stand erect but still unable to fly, they are huddling just outside their nest burrow, waiting for an adult to return with food. When Burrowing Owls hatch, they are only minimally covered with down, their eyes are closed, and they are entirely dependent upon their parents. At about two weeks of age, they become independent enough to allow both parents, not just the male, to go hunting. The owlets will make their first flights at about four weeks of age.

A period of hopping, running, and wing flapping typically precedes a young Burrowing Owl's first flight. Freshly grown, pointed primary feathers are visible at the birds' wingtips, and new dark brown secondary feathers show characteristic buff-colored spots. The developing wing and tail feathers of Burrowing Owls typically don't reach full length until shortly after the birds fledge.

American Coot

The American Coot ordinarily lays as many as twelve eggs but often doesn't start incubating until the fourth is laid. As a result, eggs that were laid earlier hatch first and all at the same time while eggs that were laid later hatch later, one at a time. Coot chicks swim well soon after hatching. When the first chicks depart the nest, one parent goes with them, leaving the other to incubate the eggs that remain. Later, when a few of the later-laid eggs hatch and these chicks depart the nest, the second parent also goes, abandoning the unhatched eggs forever.

The foraging American Coot chick below was photographed at Bear River in Utah. At least one researcher has described the combination of its orange-red forehead, orange throat, wiry ruff, and red bill as "grotesque." Yet experiments have demonstrated that the gaudy coloration plays an important role in determining how successful young coots are at attracting the attention of the parents that feed them. Coots younger than thirty days spend as much as half of their foraging time begging from their parents. As they get older, the youngsters dive more and venture farther from the adults.

Mew Gull

The Mew Gull, the smallest of North America's white-headed gulls, breeds in coastal British Columbia, the Yukon and Northwest Territories, and Alaska. Like many gulls, Mew Gulls start life outside the shell with a soft, fuzzy coat of buffy-gray down dotted with dark spots. The markings are darker on the head, and especially so on the forehead just above the mandible. Mew Gull parents are thought to rely on these markings to recognize their own chicks.

Black-bellied Whistling-Duck

Many adult birds will temporarily act as if they were ill or injured to entice a potential predator away from their eggs or young. The Black-bellied Whistling-Duck is no exception, and it uses a similar tactic when its charges are in the water. Here, on Patagonia Lake in southeastern Arizona, two adults accompany their ducklings. If a predator were to appear, one parent would swim away from the group to cause a distraction while the other would quickly lead the ducklings to cover.

American Black Duck

A variety of seeds, roots, and other parts of aquatic plants are mainstays of the American Black Duck's diet, but for the first two weeks of their lives, ducklings eat primarily insect larvae. Most ducklings are veteran overland travelers by this stage—black ducks do not lay their eggs and rear their young in the same location. Before the ducklings can start feeding, they have to walk to their wetland foraging area, which can be as far as two miles away. Led by the female, they make the landmark hike within twenty-four to twenty-seven hours of hatching, usually during twilight or at night.

American Black Ducks lay between seven and eleven eggs, all of which hatch within a few hours. Because the time between the hatching of the first egg and the last is short, the female can lead all her ducklings away from the nest without fear of leaving behind eggs that still require incubating. The adult is usually the first object that moves and makes sounds near the ducklings during the critical learning period thirteen to sixteen hours after hatching, so they imprint on her and follow her every move. The young will fledge in about two months.

Black Skimmer

Young Black Skimmers are usually in a hurry to start skimming. Just two days after taking to the air for the first time, an event that typically occurs at the ripe old age of twenty-eight to thirty days, the fledglings make their first skimming flight. Doing it just like mom and dad, the juveniles glide low over a shallow pool, dragging their knifelike lower mandible through the water in hopes of detecting a fish swimming near the surface. The birds' fishing becomes more successful with time. Their parents continue to provide food while they practice.

Like pelicans, albatrosses, and many other birds, nesting skimmers seek safety in numbers. They breed in colonies, not individually. And they go a step further: They locate their colonies within colonies of other species—usually Common, Least, Forster's, and other terns—birds that can be counted on to react immediately

and loudly to any potential predator. Their watchfulness enables the skimmers to concentrate on another important task: keeping chicks like the one above from overheating. Even as far north as Long Island, surface sand temperatures can reach 131 degrees, hot enough to kill unshaded chicks.

When Black Skimmers are about seven days old, feathers start to replace the down that covered them since hatching. By the time the birds turn three weeks old, and until they undergo another molt on their winter grounds, they look like the long-winged juvenile at right. Thinking perhaps of getting a little shut-eye, it has tucked its bill beneath buffy-edged brown feathers. When the skimmer returns in the spring, it will wear the high contrast tones of an adult: bright on its face, breast, and belly, and dark on its crown, back, and wings.

American Oystercatcher

These **American** Oystercatchers were strong enough to leave the nest **shortly** after hatching, but they're far from independent. In fact, **even** after the birds make their first flight, at about five **weeks of age**, they will still rely on their parents for food for a couple **weeks** more. The amount of time the parents must feed their **chicks** corresponds roughly with how long it takes the oyster-catchers' **unique** bills to develop fully, but there may be more to it, since **intact** family groups have been observed on the wintering grounds, **when** the young are as old as twenty-five weeks.

Black-crowned Night-Heron

Most juvenile members of the heron family look like adults, but not all of them. The Little Blue Heron, for example, starts out all-white and doesn't gain the adult's all-blue plumage until its second year. Similarly, the first-year White Ibis is largely brown. It gradually turns white in its second year. And the plumage of the juvenile Black-crowned Night-Heron, shown here, like that of the subadult Yellow-crowned Night-Heron, is mostly brown and streaked, a far cry from the bold gray, black, and white patterns of the adults.

Black-legged Kittiwake

Like other gulls in the family Laridae, the Black-legged Kittiwake
is longer from its legs to the tips of its folded wings than it is from
its legs to the tip of its bill. Unlike other gulls, the bird builds its
nest on narrow cliff ledges, some of which measure no more than
four inches from front to back—much less than the length of
the bird's folded wings. Consequently, the abundant kittiwake
often has to face the cliff, not the sea, when it is on its nest. This
black-billed juvenile and yellow-billed adult were photographed
in Newfoundland.

King Penguin

Covered only sparsely with down during the first three weeks of life, young King Penguins rely on their parents to keep them warm. Slightly older penguins look like the bird below: Covered from head to tail with thick insulating down, they can now protect themselves from the cold. When both its parents go to sea to find

food, the chick joins other juveniles in assemblages called creches, which help the young penguins stay warm and gain group protection from predators.

When King Penguin chicks are ten to thirteen months old, they replace their thick brown down with actual feathers and for the first time leave the colony and go to sea to feed themselves. The fledglings possess the dark gray-blue upperparts and white underparts of adults but typically have ear patches that are dull yellow, not the brilliant golden-orange that distinguishes adult King Penguins. The penguin above, photographed on South Georgia Island in the South Atlantic, is molting into adult plumage, a process that can take more than thirty days.

Great Crested Flycatcher

When Great Crested Flycatchers stand in the entrance to their nest cavities to feed their young, they block a portion of the light that normally shines down into the nest. Yet they can still see well enough to place food in each nestling's mouth. The chicks help by opening their bills wide, exposing their mouths' bright yellow linings and creamy white flanges. This young flycatcher is about ready to leave the nest, an event that occurs only thirteen to fifteen days after hatching. Although the bird will be able to fly when it departs, its parents will continue to bring it food for a few more weeks.

Winter Wren

Wrens originated in the New World, so scientists are curious to learn how the Winter Wren, the smallest and darkest of North America's nine wrens, also came to inhabit Eurasia. They hypothesize that it may have crossed the Bering Strait long ago. This juvenile was photographed on one of North America's westernmost points: St. Paul, a Pribilof Island in the Bering Sea. Winter Wrens on the Pribilof and Aleutian Islands are paler and larger than mainland populations.

Red-tailed Hawk

Open access to the sky and a commanding view of the surrounding countryside are absolute requirements for nesting Red-tailed Hawks. As a result, their nest sites are usually higher than those chosen by other kinds of hawks. Tall trees or trees on slopes are typical locations, but red-tails also use utility poles, building ledges, and other artificial prominences, as well as cliff ledges and giant saguaro cacti. Young hawks like these typically leave the nest six or seven weeks after they hatch but cannot fly well for another two or three weeks.

Horned Grebe

During winter along the Pacific, Atlantic, and Gulf coasts, the Horned Grebe wears a drab coat of slate-black and white feathers. Its cheeks are white, its white-tipped bill dusky. On the breeding grounds in the northern and western portions of the continent, the grebe looks dramatically different. Its flanks, chest, and neck are chestnut, its bill and cheeks are black, and a patch of elongated feathers behind each eye creates the impression of horns. The striped hatchlings in this nest are just as dazzling. The adult at right is feeding a feather to the chick on its back.

Piping Plover

A Piping Plover foraging on a beach covered with a thin layer of water will occasionally employ a clever trick to nab its prey: It will stretch out a foot and vibrate it against the sand. The rapid trembling is believed to disturb invertebrate prey items hidden beneath the surface, making them easier to see and capture. More often, the plover will simply make a series of short runs interspersed with rapid pecks. Very young chicks employ the peck-and-run foraging method immediately and graduate to foot-trembling after several days.

No longer completely covered with the creamy gray down of recently hatched birds, but still with a long way to go before they look like adults, the Herring Gull chicks at left are in the midst of a progressive molt that will produce their juvenal plumage. Black-brown spots still mark their heads, and a line of white fuzz remains on their wings, but the gull on the right has freshly grown gray-brown mantle and scapular feathers. Their pale edges give the back a scaly look. Feather sheaths on the wing promise new flight feathers soon.

The dark brown bird below, photographed on a Long Island beach, is only a few months old—old enough to fly and obtain food on its own, but still young enough to beg from an adult the way it did before it fledged. It has positioned itself directly in front of a parent, pulling its head down onto its shoulders and tossing its bill upward while giving a begging call. The parent of a juvenile that gives this display usually responds with a regurgitated meal.

Bald Eagle

The Bald Eagle is one of this continent's most successful conservation stories. Harmed by the widespread use of organochlorine pesticides, including DDT, and commonly shot and trapped, it all but disappeared throughout much of the southern and eastern United States, the Midwest and Great Plains, and southern California in the 1960s and '70s. But, like the Brown Pelican, Osprey, and Peregrine Falcon, the bird came back after the United States banned the sale and use of DDT in 1972. Today speckled immature eagles like the one at left fly in every province of Canada and every state except Rhode Island and Vermont.

The appearance of adult Bald Eagles is noticeably different from that of immature eagles. The young eagle at near right is already as big as the adult on the far right, but it will not look like the adult, with its dark body and wings and pure white head and tail, for four or even five years. Until then, the young bird will remain mostly brown with white speckles.

Species List